Goodbye Father

MAUREEN
GREEN

Goodbye
FATHER

Routledge & Kegan Paul
London and Henley

First published in 1976
by Routledge & Kegan Paul Ltd
39 Store Street,
London WC1E 7DD
and Reading Road,
Henley-on-Thames,
Oxon RG9 1EN
Printed in Great Britain by
Unwin Brothers Ltd

ISBN 0 7100 8355 6

CONTENTS

Introduction

After the hubbub that has surrounded women and their new opportunities in recent years, men are at last beginning to question and discuss the traditional roles that they have occupied in society. As far as the role of father is concerned, this attention is overdue. A major political shift in family life has taken place over the last generation. Mothers daily appear more competent and more sure of their power and their responsibilities; they head many families on their own, while father himself seems to be increasingly uncertain about what part he is expected to play.

Men today have many and severe problems in adjusting to the recent changes in family life. Yet few, at either the popular level of report and discussions in newspapers and magazines, or the professional level of research, seem to find the stresses of fatherhood a topic that merits attention. How men cope with the aspirations of women at work is recognised as a subject of some interest. But how they cope with similar women, and demanding children, at home, although more vital in some ways to a man's final happiness, is largely ignored.

Many of our reactions to the lives of our contemporaries seem to reflect an assumption that it does not matter very much if father gives up his part in the family altogether. The tolerance that is now extended to the deserting father, or to the mother who decamps with his children, by friends and business colleagues, suggests that father's contribution to family life is viewed all along as marginal. Any wife and children can be treated as perfectly able to survive without him.

The only point at which father has so far been allowed to intrude into the current debate on sexual roles is when someone has queried whether every family really needs one.

From time to time, women make well-publicised statements asserting how ably they are managing unmarried motherhood; while others reply by solemnly predicting delinquency and the severer forms of mental illness for their fatherless children. In most of these discussions, facts are few, and the participants give the impression that they are saying what they hope might come true. Yet a country with a high divorce rate and a tolerant attitude to illegitimacy needs to do more than guess at what fatherlessness can mean for the next generation.

This book is a journalist's attempt to shoot up a Very light and briefly illuminate an area that is very relevant to the current debate on male and female roles, but which is at present notable mainly for the obscurity which surrounds it. It is designed to draw together and report what is known at the moment about the problems that men are finding in fatherhood, the changes that are affecting their performance, and the necessity or otherwise of their continuing to be involved in the upbringing of the next generation.

In the course of researching this book, I have talked to many men and a few women about parenthood, and I would like to thank them all for their help, most particularly the hard-pressed divorced fathers whose experiences form the basis of chapter 6. The two chairmen of the British society for divorced fathers known as 'Families Need Fathers', Dr Alick Elithorn and Keith Parkin, have offered me every co-operation. I would also like to thank Dr Robert Andry and Dr James Hemming for the time and patience they devoted to discussing the role of contemporary fathers with me, and Dr Robert Shields for calling my attention to a number of publications that I might otherwise have missed. All of the people mentioned have guided me towards helpful facts, but the opinions expressed in the book are entirely personal to me. Those who have helped me would not agree with all of them.

I would like to thank my husband for his tolerance and support which has been a vital factor in the completion of this book. And I would also like to thank Sue Weait who has tirelessly typed, and re-typed, the manuscript. Without the help of my housekeeper, Edith Rivett, this book could not have been written at all.

Do fathers make good mothers
The changing role of the father
rise of
male headed
single
parent
families

ONE The Decline of Father

No one is taking any notice of father.

As any suburban father will testify, today's family does not fall into a respectful hush when father starts to speak. But that's only part of it. Much more ruthlessly, father is being ignored by the experts. As a topic, as a subject for research and conjecture by sociologists, by revolutionaries and journalists, father is forgotten. They are all too busy concentrating on mother.

However underprivileged women may still consider they are in many aspects of modern life, they are over-indulged in terms of the number of words devoted to them. Fifty years ago, Virginia Woolf called woman 'the most discussed animal in the universe'. Women are still an obsessive topic, the centre of all attention as they churn over their options, their rights and their duties. Millions of miles of newsprint have been devoted to just one aspect of women's lives—motherhood. By comparison, men get very little attention at all; and when they do, popular interest seems to centre on men as aggressors, as hunters. Man as family man, as father, is never on the agenda.

Yet there is plenty to investigate. Father's image has taken a plunge from the craggy dignity of an Old Testament patriarch to the television gooneries of 'Father, dear Father' in a mere half-century. The heroes of the Charge of the Light Brigade have given way in popular imagery to the buffoons of 'Dad's Army'. In the last ten years, because of permissive sexual habits, rising rates of divorce and separation and more tolerated illegitimacy, the pressure of greater ambitions from women and the assertion of some basic rights for children, the whole western system of patriarchy has already been drastically revised. And in the fifty years before that, father had begun to

1

become simply one of the family, instead of its undoubted head.

At the beginning of this century, father's power was supreme. A family ate well or badly, dressed well or badly, according to how cleverly father could push his way ahead in the world: his was the sole income. If he deserted the family, they starved. They learned only the lessons that he could pay for. If he could not afford the doctor's bills, they stayed sick or died. Father's position in the local community, his success both in business and in his social life, conferred on his wife and his children their only prestige. A woman was Mrs Smith the merchant's wife, or Miss Smith the merchant's daughter, or she was nothing. One of his wife's tasks was to bear his children, so that they might carry on his name and inherit his property. Father's judgment on moral and social questions made him priest as well as king inside his household: a role doubly underlined in those houses where family and servants assembled each morning to be led by him through prayers ending with 'Our Father . . .'

As the lone explorer into the world outside the home, he reported back its standards and expectations, and instructed his family on how they should behave to be accepted by it. His wife had to confine herself to mumbling 'if you say so, dear . . .' on hearing most of this, since she had scarcely any means of checking up on it. Father's patronage and provision of dowry kept his daughter meek. And his son had to pay attention for the essential reason that father's business was going to be his one day, and he was already working alongside his father and learning how to run it. As far as the law was concerned, all the fathers together, responsible for all their tiny realms, were the state. If a father's rights were upheld, then justice would be done. Even supposing there should be some individual in the family who should come into conflict with father, the case would be treated as an insurrection. Father was the sole guardian of his children, and a century ago he could divorce his erring wife, turn her out of the house, and forbid her ever to see his children again. The threat alone was enough to keep most women submissive.

This was a mere hundred years ago, though it sounds more like a thousand. For of the realm of this Victorian paterfamilias there now remains scarcely a shred. We count ourselves lucky that today's educated democratic family bears little resemblance to this despotism. The modern family, we like to think, is governed by consensus. The standard of living in the majority of families in Britain depends increasingly on the efforts of two adults and their dual income (most mothers still earn less than father, but the latest census revealed that, in one out of five working families, mother earns more), and the resourcefulness and early independence of their children. Their survival in a crisis, their education and their health are insured by the state. Everyone's prestige depends on their individual achievement, and not on reflected glory from any other member of the family; Mrs Smith is the social worker who is married to a lawyer, and their daughter is Miss Smith who is at art school. Education specialists predict that the social status of the children will depend more, in the long run, on the educational levels attained by the *mother*. Moral and social questions are the subject of constant debate and conflict, in which the generations are pleased if they can find an area of mutual understanding. Each member of the family sorts out for himself what is socially acceptable behaviour in his own circle, be it among his peer group at nursery school, fellow students at college, alongside cameramen in the television studios where mother works, in the sales office where father puts in a long day. His son does not feel obliged to pay too much attention to father's opinions and instructions since he is bound for a career in computer technology that did not exist in his father's day, and he will have to spend patient hours explaining to Dad what it is all about. As Herbert Marcuse[1] writes, 'in the struggle between the generations the sides seem to be shifted; the son knows better.' And the law is by and large concerned with the rights of individuals—men, women and children equally. Should the family split up, the courts will try to decide the custody of the children in accordance with the children's best interests and welfare. As for God, in whose image father once felt he was created, he has, with more or less regret, been declared dead. Without a venerable male figure in heaven to back him up, father himself feels fatherless.

And wherever he looks he sees masculine values at a discount. There are those who believe, like Gordon Rattray Taylor,[2] that we live in a 'matrist' age, a period in history when mother's way of looking at the world is the overriding influence. The 'patrist' centuries that father dominated were traditionally preoccupied with property and position; they were restrictive about sexual behaviour and nudity, esteemed discipline, down-graded women and hesitated before scientific research that might meddle with the achievements of their forefathers. When the maternal point of view dominates, however, as Rattray Taylor argues that it does today, civilisation concentrates on solving social problems such as famine relief and bad housing; society is noticeably egalitarian, permissive about sexual experiment and nudity, appreciates the talents of both sexes, admires spontaneity, and is always ready to assist 'progress', no matter how much it may undermine traditional values. So all-pervading is the maternal view of life today, that even sons run off to join the Peace Corps or work for Oxfam, rather than to be soldiers or to extend the boundaries of Empire. So father has perhaps the additional problem of being father in what is already the century of the common woman.

Whether we talk about 'patrism' and the broad sweep of history, paternalism and international relations, or automatic respect for father in the family, all are equally out of fashion.

The despotic power of father has been struck down. The old patriarch has disappeared and other members of the family have gained in strength and independence at his expense. Even father's sexual mastery has been undermined. His wife has acquired the right to orgasm, as well as the right to vote. Father now feels an obligation to satisfy his wife sexually, which may be more of a burden than nineteenth-century pressures for sexual restraint. His wife has the power to decide when she wishes to conceive. She is the one who takes the Pill. If her husband proves infertile, she can even turn to AID. In family quarrels, mother may today be the aggressor and blackmailer, threatening to take the children away. Now that father has been rendered harmless, his past supremacy is often referred to with sentiment and nostalgia. Millions in Britain and other European countries fell for the charm of what critic Cyril Connolly called 'the great frieze of father figures' in the television serialisation of *The Forsyte Saga*. It is easy enough to miss the old man, now that he is safely gone.

For gone he is. Women and children have won their new freedoms partly at his expense, but in giving up some of his awesome privileges, father has also shifted some of his burdens. In letting his wife share in earning the family income, he has reduced some of his traditional anxiety and achieved greater flexibility to take bold risks in his own career. In agreeing to be more tolerant about his wife's sexual life, to abandon age-old ideas of the need to keep women as chaste reproductive vessels, father has himself partially escaped from the strains of strict monogamy to experience a little more of the sexual variety that he always pined for. The number of men who would now enjoy playing the role of stern Victorian paterfamilias is probably very few. Most would consider it absurd. They much prefer being a modern father. *If only they could be a little more certain what that is.* For the Victorian situation did have one advantage for father that he would indeed have liked to hang on to: in those days, he knew what he was for. Many a modern father has begun to wonder. What is he actually supposed to do? 'From time to time', confesses one father nervously, 'I find that all the family look round at me as if expecting me to solve something or be something, but I'm certainly not sure what.'

Surely, there must be a contribution that father can make to the family that is equal to mother's, but different? The Victorian father knew that he took final responsibility for his entire household, but he never concerned himself with the details, like changing nappies. That was mother's job. But mother is now doing two jobs, one outside the house and one inside. Her problems are strenuous but they are positive. Father is in a more negative situation. Should he balance up mother's dual role by involving himself more in looking after the children, and find a stronger domestic part for himself? In fact, the modern husband and father is today more willing to give a hand with baby's bath and bottle feeds, and toddler's bed-time stories than ever before, as sociologists John and Elizabeth Newson[3] have charted. But is such 'helping' father's essential role? If father gives infant feeds and changes nappies, does he give his children the benefit of a good father or of an auxiliary, male, mother? Isn't there something he should be doing that mother can't?

In practice, no matter how senior a breadwinner he is all week, father tends to check in as mother's personal assistant at the weekend. In most families it is still accepted that mother is running the house, even though she is out of it more and more.

So father 'helps' by chauffeuring the children to their parties on Saturday afternoon, by getting in the extra supermarket shopping and performing any other task mother thinks up. Everyone is conscious that the family need to stick together, not just to eat and keep a roof over their heads, but for their greatest personal satisfactions. And personal relations—the supervision of happiness—is the department where mother finds it easy to assume the part of expert. Professionals and laymen today agree that mother is now the centre of the family. Social anthropologist Edmund Leach has pronounced 'the contemporary British stereotype of the monogamous, neolocal [that is, two-generation] elementary family has a markedly "matrifocal" emphasis—the king-pin of the structure tends to be "mum" rather than "dad".' Johnny Speight, writer and creator of 'Till Death Do Us Part', which features television's awful father, the scorned and scornful Alf Garnett, says, 'In the average house the kids know who's running it. Father pays the bills, but Mum decides what goes on.'

From the children's point of view what mother does is obvious; father's achievements are a remote mystery. Yet they take up so much of his time. In many professional families in Britain today, it is an accepted fact of life that father is a lavish provider, but that it takes all his waking hours and most of his interest to keep in this position. Very early in life, the children are apt to doubt that father *has* to work to keep them all; he obviously prefers to. In the United States, father has long had an intense relationship with a second 'family' in his place of business, among colleagues who share in his achievements and crises and from whom he seems to get his greatest personal satisfaction. In his biological family, he appears from time to time like Father Christmas, distributing gifts after business trips. Mother has to bring up the children almost on her own.

This devouring business pattern has now spread across the Atlantic. The time and attention of many men in Europe has for some while been similarly claimed by the organisations they work for, but the effect that this has had on our personal lives is only now beginning to be pinpointed. Surveying 500 homes on a private housing estate in London, sociologist Dr Gaynor Cohen spotted the phenomenon of 'the absent husband', and concluded that business schedules effectively prevent many men from spending much time with their children. 'There are a growing number of middle-class families where the husband is forced—through career pressures—to be away from home for substantial lengths of time. As a result the men play a far less pronounced role in the family than the assumptions of equality have led us to expect.'[4]

Wives and mothers who cannot accept that work comes first in the lives of such husbands are sometimes discarded in favour of enthusiastic female colleagues who seem to promise that they really know how to back up an ambitious man. Woe betide such a second wife who suddenly decides that she, too, would like to be a mother, and that her spouse should somehow find his second batch of children more interesting than the first and give them some of his attention. She may have to learn that although her husband is economically able to provide for the two families that he has engendered, the emotional support will not be supplied. The race he has entered, to win a living for all of them, will leave him scant time for fathering—whatever that might be.

The dismay that can hit the sons of our century's alienated fathers has been bitterly expressed by American novelist Stephen Koch. Speaking for his own generation, which grew to adulthood amid the cultural revolution of the 1960s, he asks:[5]

Who, among those fiery sons, really connected with his father; who even knew, let alone admired what the father did in that invisible city of his? Fatherhood meant delivering, or not delivering, checks. It meant not being around, or being unwelcome when around. It meant either shouting, or that soul-crushing silence most deeply installed in the soul of any red-blooded American boy: Dad mute behind his newspaper. Dad losing an argument. Dad standing alone watering the lawn, wooden as a dead post—while inside the household lived that real life in which he didn't count. Fatherhood, and to that degree manhood, meant being feared, or ignored, or despised, or pitied, or hated . . .

The one ambition such a father passed on to his son was never to grow up like him. ' "Be a man," the tender initiate was told. *That* man? *Never* again,' Stephen Koch concludes.

Father's role has shrunk so drastically that it is no longer obvious how it can be worn with confidence. And in many cases it has become quite invisible. Every year an increasing number of families make do without father at all. The National Council for One-Parent Families represents the needs of 500,000 fatherless families, involving over a million children. Many of our children are growing up with only a remote idea of what a father is. Father is disappearing from the scene and the reason is simple: marriage is increasingly breaking down and there is no role for him outside it. The unmarried father, the father who has just seen his divorced wife awarded custody of the children, is in practical and emotional terms cut off. His life centres on what would be the men's compound in the primitive village, where work and drink and transient sex are to be had, but real access to the future is denied.

'It's a farce to say that I am a father', says one ex-husband whose wife and children moved to Canada, six thousand miles away, when his marriage split up. An energetic woman has just moved into a south London suburb with her four children, after her husband walked out on her two years ago. Since then, the children's father travels several hundred miles one Sunday a month to take the children out for the day. That, and the maintenance money of course, are his total contribution. An attractive girl in broadcasting, with an elegant St John's Wood flat, has just decided that having passed her thirtieth birthday, she has reached the time of life and the income to start a family. It's just that the man she fancies as a father, she does not really want to marry. But she is going to go ahead with a baby anyway. Even a decade ago, the divorcee and the unmarried mother would have been viewed solely as stern social problems under the stereotyped headings of 'broken homes' and 'illegitimacy'. Now their lives—admittedly not without problems—are dignified by the title 'One-Parent Families' and government bodies are studying their worries with a view to sustaining their family life, not punishing or preventing it.

When starvation and stigma no longer lie in wait for the fatherless, and mothers on their own earn respect from their friends and the state for their heroic efforts, fatherhood is not what it was. The pendulum that has swung away from father and unseated him from his Victorian throne has not stopped at the creation of a modern democratic family. It is still swinging. And father is beginning to appear as a luxurious but optional extra.

In the general shake-up that marriage and the family are

undergoing at present, the prophets and activists are all pointing to the death of the family as the way ahead; other groups, be they communes or kibbutz, are envisaged that will help the individual survive better. But in practice, when the crunch comes, when marriages dissolve or individuals decide to avoid them, when communes split up and 'godfathers' disappear, women and children are increasingly solving their practical problems by retaining—or returning to—an earlier institution: the family without father.

When husbands and wives are in prolonged conflict, very few today would advise them to stay together 'for the sake of the children'. The recommended way to escape the strain is for the couple to split up. Since psychologists have emphasised the importance of the mother-child bond above all else, judges almost invariably award custody of the children to the mother. Father is granted 'reasonable access' to the children, but if mother decides to move to another house or another country, or pack the sons off to boarding school, he may seldom see any of them. It is now quite often the 'erring wife' who sees father off the premises. In practical terms, what this means is that the family loses father.

To the disappointment of many leaders of the women's liberation movement who rightly pinpoint children as the burden that holds women back, having children is part of the life ambition of most women—even the most talented and independent. 'I think I could have survived without children. But I doubt if Mary could', said Alexander Plunket-Greene recently, explaining the arrival of a son in their middle age. Mary is Mary Quant, the energetic head of an international fashion empire. Many other strongly independent women are surprised at how much they do want children. But not all are able to accept the old bargain between the sexes that marriage still upholds. While a new bargain is being worked out, they plan a one-parent family.

Even if it is a struggle for the separated or divorced mother to survive, even if only a tiny minority of single women can make anything like a success of a planned one-parent family, their actions raise a thicket of threatening questions around the role of father. The head of the family is remembered to be historically the last one to have joined it—and therefore perhaps aptly the first to leave.

Most of us still imagine that Adam and Eve or some couple were the first unit in human history. In our personal lives, it is true we usually begin by finding an individual who seems right as a companion and lover, and then focus on the idea of becoming parents. But in human evolution, it was surely the other way round. Copulation and reproduction were always with us; but the idea of two parents came a long, long time after. And came only to homo sapiens. In scanning the habits and instincts of animals, to work out how they relate to us humans, recent observers have brought us back to a realisation that nature's family consists in the main of mothers and children. In the wild, the male copulates and runs. While the closest affection can exist between a great chimpanzee matriarch like Flo and her numerous adult children and grandchildren (observed in Africa through many years of busy family life by scientist Jane Goodall), Flo's sexual partners did not stay around for long, and took no interest in her offspring. In many of the animal species, including some of the primates, the male considers young infants to be merely irritating, and in some cases edible. As Elaine Morgan reminds us, 'We tell our children tales about a cosy household of "Father Bear, Mother Bear and Baby Bear", oblivious of the fact that Father Bear would certainly gobble up Baby Bear on sight, if Mother Bear didn't give the child some rigorous training in shinning up a tree trunk before letting him loose on his own.'[6]

But at some crucial point in human development, nature's easy-going family of mother and children acquired a father who would not eat the children, but help to rear them. According to many anthropologists, finding a convincing part for the male in the human family drama took imagination and effort. And the children the human male first learned to provide for were not necessarily his biologically. Even today, there are primitive societies where the mother's brother is expected to be the male protector. But when at some point in history the biological link of paternity was discovered and understood it changed the entire outlook. The significance and precariousness of the male position, once fully apprehended, led to the invention of the family. Fatherhood became an ambition, a dream, involving ideas of creation and immortality. Yet if men wished to become fathers, with children they could recognise as their own, they had to become husbands. And if women were to be persuaded into marriage, and given in marriage between men, they had to be offered and controlled by economic rewards; a woman and her children would be fed and clothed and accorded a status appropriate to the husband and father's social position, in return for promising that her children were indeed his. The unprovable nature of paternity was always a nightmare; much of the history of the relations of men and women is the history of men over-reacting with fright at the tenuous character of fatherhood. (The prime example of male fright is found in the law of a number of Continental countries, including France and Italy, with regard to the birth of the illegitimate, where the child can be entered into the birth registers as the son of a particular father, with mother unknown. 'M'ignota' is a favourite Italian obscenity addressed to those who are presumed not to know the name of their mother. The obviousness of motherhood, the uncertainty of paternity, had to be denied at all costs, no matter how absurd.) Partly from fright, father insisted on dominating his household; and only in this century has he been popularly suspected and accused of overplaying his hand.

The usefulness of harnessing masculine energy to the role of family provider however soon became obvious. The division of labour between the sexes allowed patriarchal societies to make the fastest progress. That the need to supervise, control and downgrade the contribution of women embittered the relations between the sexes, seemed perhaps a small price to pay. 'Love as a relation between men and women was ruined', Bertrand Russell has argued, 'by the desire to make sure of the legitimacy of children.' But something more than mere survival was assured for the human race and mankind made a great leap forward. The more elaborate the material life he supplied, the more essential father seemed. Until finally, there he was at the head of the Victorian table, carving the turkey he had so capably provided. The solidity of his position economically disguised the fact that he was, more than anything else, an idea. 'Human fatherhood', anthropologist Margaret Mead was one of the first to suggest,[7] 'is a social invention.' It is not a biological instinct like motherhood. 'Men have to learn to want to provide for others, and this behaviour, being learned, is rather fragile and can disappear rather easily under social conditions that no longer teach it effectively.' Like any lesson, it is learned more thoroughly by some individuals and social groups than by others; and there have always been men who could not learn it at all. In a fatherless family, it is possible that the lesson cannot be taught. But a deserting father is running out on a social obligation that he has been conditioned and has promised to perform; a deserting mother is cutting up some part of her own self. This difference, when it is unrecognised, makes women judge men harshly, and consider them inferior. As the heroine of a Margaret Drabble novel remembers severely,[8] 'she had once thought it an indictment upon the whole sex, the ease with which men would abandon their offspring.'

In view of the fragility and confusion of father's role, and the rising tide of the fatherless, the benefits and disadvantages of father seem in need of reappraisal. He is the most ambiguous figure in the future of the human family. The role that started out as a bright idea and led to patriarchy has now reached a low ebb. Is father's lessening intervention in the family to be accepted, until he disappears altogether? Or can father be re-invented? Father, for the moment, is an endangered species to be preserved, if at all, only by careful thought and planning.

TWO NON-STICK MARRIAGE

The original preservation society for father was marriage. This was the institution that offered him a part to play, responsibilities and satisfactions. But marriage today is no longer an institution. It is a relationship. And it is a relationship in which one of the partners has changed out of all recognition, and both start out with and develop demands and expectations that have never been envisaged before.

Marriage is now the central adult adventure. More people are getting into it than ever before, more people are getting out of it than ever before, more people are doing it more than once. Everybody talks about it, everybody writes about it. Marriage is considered the ideal vessel for mutual exploration and discovery. But it is not expected to last forever. Matrimony has become what one journalist ruefully refers to as 'non-stick' marriage!

And marriage begins to show most signs of strain once it is expected to carry children. The contraceptive Pill is hailed as having separated sex and reproduction. It has also separated marriage and reproduction. The sexual-family strands of married life are no longer entwined, but in fact are beginning to fray and unravel. We are now in such a muddle about marriage that it works worst for those it was originally designed to sustain: parents and children. Because of the confusion in our minds about what marriage may be expected to do for us, husbands can now accuse their wives and mothers of their children of not being sufficiently 'exciting', and women can blame their husbands and the fathers of their children for their own 'intellectual isolation'. Such fault-finding in any earlier age would have been considered ludicrously irrelevant. Marriages are breaking down so often (one in four marriages now ends in divorce) because we are no longer certain about what we expect marriage to supply.

On the one hand, marriage has been raised to the level of the ultimate and most enriching of all relationships, and a good marriage is generally considered one of the achievements of a healthy and successful individual. On the other, every individual's right to self-development in what Alex Comfort calls today's 'society of greater personal expectations' means that more and more of us feel that we are allowed to keep trying for real happiness; opt for a way of life that will keep us growing, broaden and change our relationships, including our marriages, when we no longer find them satisfying. Fewer and fewer are prepared just to sit out their lives and endure their mistakes. Now that we live so long, any marriage, happy or miserable, could conceivably last for half a century. One young divorced woman relates: 'my parents were never happily married but they stuck it out. Perhaps they couldn't see any alternative. But when I felt that I had outgrown my young husband, I could see an alternative. I know that there is time for me to start a new life.'

So it is partly because ideals of 'human potential' are so high, and marriage is expected to fulfil so many of them, that an increasing number of marriages crack under the pressure. But many other aspects of the way we think and feel today make marriage harder to hold together.

We are not really such a materialistic society, despite the constant breast-beating that we indulge in to expiate our guilty pleasure in the affluence that surrounds us. An increasing number of us are lucky enough to view our work not just as grinding toil that makes us a living but as a chance to express our talents and add interest to our lives. Nearly all of us look forward to marriage, not as a device for placing a roof over our heads, but as a source of emotional enrichment. In the present century, and only in the west, most marriages are now made for reasons other than securing some adjoining land, welding alliances between clans, joining businesses or providing for impoverished sons and daughters. Few today need to consider whether a future marriage will bring them more relatives to work in the fields, or more finance for a family business. Our affluence makes us free to choose our partners for less worldly satisfactions; but the intangible benefits that we long for are much less easy to guarantee. The very fact that a woman does not have to regard her spouse as a meal-ticket, or think of him as a good 'catch', has given marriage a less brutal, but also less firm, basis.

Our values today are equally high-minded and unhelpful. We do not award very high marks to individuals for impeccable role-playing. A 'devoted mother', a 'benevolent father', a 'dutiful daughter', a 'loyal wife' are today regarded as absurd cardboard characters. Individuals are expected to value authentic, personal feelings and reactions; someone who simply feels what he thinks he is expected to feel is regarded as a predictable bore. We are all existentialists now—or try to be. In her novel *The Nice and the Good*, Iris Murdoch has depicted individuals who live mainly by learning the rules and their roles and abiding by them. They are 'nice people'. She contrasts them with other men and women who do what they must, live as they feel, ignoring the rule book. Like all saints, these characters sometimes make life difficult for those around them. However, they are judged 'good' people. But perhaps we have to make compromises, even in virtue? Mere niceness can sometimes keep a marriage going through a crisis. Those who frequently refuse to do what is expected make interesting companions but possibly unreliable husbands and wives. Marriage may need everyone to be willing at least to try on the traditional roles for size from time to time.

Self-sacrifice is also out of favour, and self-development in. Those who live their lives for others arouse suspicion rather than admiration, and their motives are unflatteringly discussed. Others who chart an increasingly demanding and achieving course for themselves through life are lauded for their creativity and vigour; that they may have lost their intimate companions on the way is accepted as an inevitable risk. What is totally unacceptable is any plea for self-restraint or self-discipline; our loftiest ideal is of the freedom of the individual. A society where every individual shall be free to enjoy life to the limits of their capacity, to change and grow according to his or her own potential, is the blueprint for the new Jerusalem. Whether that society of 'egalitarian hedonism', as Lionel Trilling defines it, can contain marriage as it has previously been known is increasingly open to question.

Both sexes are on the look-out for partners who will not

expect them to do any of the things that their parents did. Women most obviously are flexing their muscles, stretching their minds and seeking out challenges that their mothers shied away from. The fact that marriage now houses two whole adults, instead of one and a half as before, makes life more complicated. Despite traditional fears, however, wives who continue to follow their ambitions outside the home do not seem to drive husbands away. If women are alert and satisfied, they are easier to live with. But when men do not realise that women have changed, there is trouble. Jack Dominian, head of the Marital Research Unit at the Central Middlesex Hospital is of the opinion that 'nine out of ten divorces in the first few years of marriage are caused by the husband's limited view of his wife. She feels imprisoned by his view of her.' Many young women who were brought up to expect that marriage would supply everything they could ever want for a happy life soon find themselves brooding 'is this all?' after a few years' experience of the real thing. The ideas they brought to marriage were either wild fantasies of being 'happy ever after' or crippling feelings of the duty to be perfect housewives and mothers; in throwing out these second-rate notions, many abandoned their marriages at the same time. 'I really thought that marriage to Joe would make me wildly happy. I was crazy about him. But all I discovered was that most of the time I could no longer do what I wanted,' says one recent convert to the women's movement. 'When my son arrived, I thought that I would feel this wonderful fulfilment that you read about in the magazines. But I couldn't move without that child. I was absolutely trapped. Marriage and children—it's just a con.'

Not all women became feminists in such a fit of sulks. But the Women's Liberation Movement has often been attacked as a marriage-breaker. Movement defenders claim it simply let in a little light and started the re-think. Betty Friedan, former head of the National Organisation for Women, asserts: 'If divorce has increased by 1,000 per cent, don't blame the women's movement. Blame the obsolete sex roles on which our marriages were based.'

Yet marriage is showing itself able to bend before some of the new breezes. Instead of the firm vows that were once heard at every marriage ceremony, including such memorable promises as 'forsaking all other' and 'till death us do part', many young couples today marry, if indeed they do marry, with a complicated commitment to each other which may very carefully omit such time-honoured undertakings while seeking out wholly new ones. As Professor Jessie Bernard relates in *The Future of Marriage*, many Americans today find it somewhat tiresome to be invited to a wedding, since they frequently have to endure a long dissertation on 'our relationship' by the young people involved instead of the conventional marriage service. As an example of the very difficult promises that some young people do make to each other she quotes a recent wedding 'commitment':

> Both of us commit ourselves to 1) continue to grow each in his or her unique way; 2) retain future choices about our relationship, recognising that the risks of growth include the risks of growing apart; 3) give room for the process of growing, being patient with no-growth plateaus, being 'there' when it's painful, giving space for the bursts of joy; 4) provide a climate that stimulates and invites growing—confronting without judging, sensing when the most help is no help; 5) take risks of self-exposure, confrontation, pain, shame, also risks of joy, fun, play; 6) respect differences of belief or viewpoint, without requiring agreement but expecting a curiosity to understand, or acceptance.

It is a tall order. This young pair were hoping for a great deal from each other. What they were obviously not expecting or promising was permanence or sexual fidelity. Their commitment might be wholly admirable, if the couple also agreed not to have children. But there is no recognition in their promises that one or other of them might in the future wish to make some 'choice' that was incompatible with the choices of a dependent three-year-old; that in giving room for the processes of 'growth' in each other they might be making the growth of a young child more hazardous. It is an agreement that ignores parenting altogether.

Yet this commitment ceremony, far-out as it must seem to some, only recognises in an extreme and candid form what many others look for in their marriages. 'You're blocking my development' is probably one of the most final of present-day accusations against a spouse, even if it is seldom so phrased.

And the block is frequently most resented if it presents itself in the form of sexual fetters. One of the extra pressures that every modern marriage has to bear is that brought about by greater freedom and higher expectations in sexual life. Not only have we abandoned the belief that human beings are naturally monogamous. Many of our new ideals of self-development are centred on sexuality itself. Sexual attraction is the single most important force that brings a couple together and ignites a new marriage, though many other slower-burning fuels may keep it going later on. Though a man and woman singling each other out for marriage also test each other for compatibilities in many other ways—searching out qualities that will complement their own and hoping for aims and goals in life that will be similar—one of the key satisfactions hoped for is a satisfying sexual life. But here again marriage seems to have been put on the defensive.

Though many of its more exhibitionist moments now seem to be over, it is still true that we have been living through a sexual revolution. What the practical aftermath of that revolution now amounts to is that single people today feel that they may go ahead with full sexual intercourse once they are involved with each other, while in the past the majority of them would have had to stop short at some form of 'petting'. They are able to do what any healthy young couple in love have always wanted to do. They can also settle into semi-permanent arrangements of living together, while their emotional attachments last, without causing as much as a raised eyebrow. The reason they are enjoying this unprecedented freedom is easy to see. For the first time, there is a 100 per cent effective contraceptive available in the shape of the Pill. And it is available to women and therefore reassures the traditionally more hesitant partner. A censorious society is no longer standing by to reproach a girl for losing her virginity before marriage, with the suggestion that she is lowering her market value. It is even recognised that a girl's later marriage may benefit from the wisdom she has acquired in earlier sexual and emotional encounters. Women have reason to feel freer than ever before.

And beyond that, many now believe that their happiness is dependent on their exercising that freedom. Sex has become the thread that we follow through the maze of self-development. Over the last decade, a lively minority of the young have plunged on with their sexual experiments, tract in hand. The students of the 1960s who marched across campuses with banners that read 'Make Love not War' were fuelled not just by their own natural young energy, but by the ideas of Wilhelm Reich and Herbert Marcuse. Reich, a psychoanalyst expelled from Freud's original circle for his revolutionary opinions, predicted every ill, from cancer to neurosis to war, for those who could not obtain regular, satisfactory sex. The function of the orgasm, taught Reich, was to preserve health. The man or woman achieving full sexual satisfaction felt well in body, found it possible to face the real world and not retreat into fantasy, and in this mood was not prone to use his energy in aggressive attacks on others. At the same time, Herbert Marcuse, philosopher and teacher at the University of California, was adopted as a prophet by many of his pupils' generation for his proposals that the achievement of sexual freedom was a necessary precondition to any achievement of political freedom. Sexually liberated men or women can find the path to liberty and happiness; the sexually cowed find it easy to bend the knee to authoritarian government and to channel their energies into the labour force. For both Reich and Marcuse marriage is a dead loss. From Reich's point of view, because it leads within a few years to sexual monotony and makes the kind of satisfaction he envisages impossible. And for Marcuse, because marriage is seen as a control on the sexual instinct, and an instrument of oppression.

Though many young people have never heard of Reich or Marcuse, most behave as if they had—finding that their built-in conviction that sex is good for them has somehow come to be tolerated rather more by the world around them. Though many young women do not take the Pill, most behave as if they do, copying the relaxed sexual manners of their more far-sighted friends. As a result, the lives of the young are freer and easier than anything we have known before. Even when the unforeseen occurs—an unplanned pregnancy—the escape routes, the choices before the couple concerned, are not as cramping as they once were. The shotgun marriage is not the immediate and only course of action. The unmarried father can frequently be involved in the general concern and handled with tact. If the pregnancy is unwanted as well as unplanned, abortion is available (though sometimes the emotional cost is considerable). If the girl decides to go ahead with the baby but remain unmarried, friends and neighbours may even rally round and present her with gifts rather than treat her as an outcast. The unmarried father may drift away or be made to feel superfluous, but the mother and her baby will be allowed to feel that they belong.

The real pioneers in all the new sexual and social situations are women. For the first time, they have found that they can begin to experiment and think and criticise and wonder about what satisfies them. They have the education, they have a sense of themselves as significant individuals, they have a pay-packet, and they have the Pill. They do not need to strike an economic bargain with their partners on approaching every emotional or sexual encounter. They have not had to ask themselves the primitive questions that have always guided women: 'Is he a man who would stand by me? Would he be a reliable provider? Would he be a responsible father?' The majority of men have welcomed women's more easy-going attitudes to sexual experience. Though men have always previously insisted on female chastity as a paternity certificate, most today seem to regard the Pill as sufficient. (Whether that confidence is misplaced is another matter. A blood-group survey in one town in southern England accidentally turned up the information that in about 30 per cent of families in that town, there was at least one child who could not have been fathered by the husband. The survey was dropped in embarrassed dismay.) We are fast approaching the land that Alex Comfort first sighted, where chastity is more closely connected in the popular mind with malnutrition than with purity.

Looking back on the last decade, and the new freedom of choice before so many men and women, some remarkable developments can already be seen. Women seem to have made some hard discoveries. A mere half dozen years ago all the emphasis was on a woman's right to enjoy her sexual life exactly as a man. As much sex as you want was the recipe for a liberated life. Women started to say 'yes'. They said they needed the experience. That of course they knew it wouldn't last. That they felt free to move on. And they agreed that jealousy was a sign of immaturity (more difficult to say, that last one). And finally, like Caroline Brown, a twenty-four-year-old London designer who admitted that she and the young man she was living with 'had both been through the mill a bit', they came to the conclusion: 'we both know it isn't possible to be sexually faithful to one person for ever. But sex isn't that important. What I would like is to have a child at some point in my life'.

That was a well-trod path, from 'sex is the path to liberty' right through to 'sex is not that important'. A whole generation of girls suddenly felt that they had been had. In dreaming their way out to a new frontier, they woke up back in the slave camp. They found themselves in and out of bed, not only with men they loved or men they liked. In the words of one American college girl, 'not only have we been sleeping with guys we don't love, but with guys we positively can't stand. What are we doing it for?'[1]

Young women who had started off proud not to be using their sexuality to strike bargains, wanting to use it for their own pleasure and growth and development, began to find that mere sleeping around made them miserable. There was no pleasure for them unless they were highly selective and able to enjoy a complicated, loving relationship with their sexual partners. There was not much growth and development unless they were able to think about a day when they could have children. A lot of them began to realise that the old bourgeois bargain, symbolised by 'that triumph of kitsch, the white wedding', as Germaine Greer calls it, had a point. Possibly their grandmothers and mothers had never taken the lies and fantasies of 'romance' seriously and had always hated the fact that their personal liberty was utterly curtailed, but at least conventional marriage offered them their first choices: companionship and children. The new freedom often made these basics seem very hard to achieve.

A number of feminists now attack the recent 'sexual revolution' as a male plot. For when women began to say that they were ashamed of the old bargains, that they were too independent to be husband-hunters, men took them at their word. Shulamith Firestone, a leading American feminist, writes bitterly: 'By convincing women that the old female games and demands were despicable, unfair, prudish, old-fashioned, puritanical and self-destructive, a new reservoir of available females was created to expand the tight supply of goods

available for traditional sexual exploitation, disarming women
of even the little protection they had so painfully acquired.'[2]
But no plot was needed. Women had genuinely outgrown one
bargain. And they had not worked out a new one. They were
doubly vulnerable; and the men were doubly confused. Yet
there had been some gains.

But every improvement for the unmarried, has made the
married more edgy. As Margaret Drabble says, 'Whereas young
unmarried people do live now with a more relaxed, permissive
attitude towards sex, marriage itself has become increasingly
difficult, strained, tense and neurotic.' The married no longer
feel that they represent the only possible way of life; their
pattern is simply one of a number of alternatives. Nor do they
feel any certainty that their marriages will last for ever; they
live with doubt.

The repercussions are enormous. As a society, we have not
yet begun to think out the consequences of impermanent
marriage. Very few who study the lives of working mothers pay
any attention to their motives; yet the temporary nature of
modern marriage causes many young mothers to feel that they
must work to keep up their only long-term security. At some
time in the future they may have to take over the full
responsibility for their children; their standard of living then,
and that of their teenagers, may depend on how soon they
returned to work after the birth of their babies. Child guidance
experts may have doubts about working mothers, but mothers
may have doubts about their marriages.

And the main reason for their insecurity is that marriage has
not finally settled their sexual and emotional fate. Those who
lived tolerantly or adventurously as single individuals now try
to do so as husbands and wives. This permissive climate is one
that has been enjoyed in the past by some classes and by some
countries, but always in circumstances where divorce was
forbidden. In earlier times, no matter what love affairs were
indulged in alongside marriage, they remained alongside
marriage, so that social stability was never threatened. Today
for the first time, young couples marry and then continue to
shop around. Love affairs lead to social disarray. Everyone lives
with marital jitters, but especially women. For once they have
small children, they have neither the opportunity nor the
energy nor the alibis necessary to compete for sexual

adventure; they find themselves increasingly dependent.

Their dependency is not something innate in the nature of women, but a creation of marriage. As Professor Jessie Bernard has proved in detail, it is men who flourish in the married situation. The reason that married men so often seem to be floating buoyantly in life's waters while their wives go under is due not to their wives' inability to swim, but to the fact that the women are often swimming half-submerged with the men on their backs. Professor Bernard's surveys reported in *The Future of Marriage* have shown that the healthiest citizens in the United States today, both physically and mentally, are single women; the least healthy, single men, whether unmarried or widowers. But marriage reverses this, and the married man becomes the best of insurance bets, while his wife shows every sign of physical and mental strain. As Professor Bernard succinctly sums up: 'Being a housewife makes women sick'.

Every wife soon finds that she is putting a lot of effort into marriage. Once children are born, her narrow domestic cell becomes even more demanding and difficult to run. The tougher and more complex it gets, the more it interests, involves and exhausts her. Many women have always gloried in this, but now just as many resent it. To the traditional complaints of men that marriage does not really suit their natures are added women's accusations that marriage inevitably cramps their style. Many a young woman finds that marriage and children exclude her from the kind of ideas and the kind of people that she was educated and trained to enjoy. She is removed from the controlled world of work, with its more predictable prizes, to the uncontrollable and subtle rewards of private living. Her daily round may become monotonous as well as satisfying, isolated from adults as well as warmly involved in children. 'I don't think I ever quite realised', says one former career woman now at home with two small children, 'that the conscious happy decision of mine to have children would lead to me spending so much of my life in the kitchen. Sometimes, when I am clearing up the egg yolk and ketchup, I think back to the business lunches that I used to have and I can't believe that I am the same person. Opting for motherhood too often means opting to be a drudge.'

It is at this point, when she has become firmly committed to but constrained by the family, when she begins to feel she is only half the person she used to be, that many a wife suddenly notices that her partner is looking very smug and self-satisfied. He feels twice the person he was before. And with reason: not only does he have one woman propping him up at home; he has found another outside.

Sexual jealousy splits communes and undermines marriages. Even quite liberated women can get very disturbed about such an old-fashioned thing as adultery. And for many it produces despair. Whether a woman sees herself as increasingly downtrodden or as a tower of strength, the more educated she is, the more she has been used to a life in which she was treated as a significant person with equal rights to equal opportunities for everything, including sex, the less will she be able to tolerate the situation. For the woman in charge of small children, 'open' marriage simply leaves her feeling draughtily exposed. If she is the only one taking the family seriously, she begins to feel that she may as well do it on her own. At this point, she has neither the energy nor the desire to compete sexually. Juggling house, children and work is a sufficient burden, without a subversive husband.

As novelist Eva Figes once concluded:[3]

what seems to happen in marriage is that you start off equal. Then the man who is at work and moving around all day meeting people all the time has the opportunities to be unfaithful. If the woman is at home looking after small children there is too much resentment for them to become friends. *He* gets involved with other people, *she* doesn't. It's always been like this for women really. The only difference now is that they don't have to put up with it.

Like Eva Figes, they end up with their children, but without their children's father. Whether wives disapprove of their husbands' adultery or envy him his opportunities for varied living does not make much practical difference. The marriage that started with sexual attraction ends with sexual attraction—to someone else. Wives decide, or are forced, to conserve their energies for themselves and their children. And father goes his separate way.

The couple without children, the couple whose children are already grown up, do not experience these tensions to the same degree. They can both continue with their work, their interests and achievements. They can frequently continue with their equal balance of affections and resentments, loyalties and infidelities. But it is the couple with young children, the couple that we have always thought marriage was originally designed for, who today find the situation increasingly intolerable. The sexual and family strands of married life are no longer entwined, but quickly unwinding. Our new permissiveness has brought greater freedom to those who were already poised to use it; but it has removed social support from parenthood. As Carl Levett the psychologist sums up:[4] 'One of the obvious and gnawing dilemmas of the contemporary . . . scene is the side affects that accelerated individualisation has had on parent-child relationships.'

The freedoms we are busily claiming for ourselves as individuals would already have brought our society into even greater confusion had we not been able to rely on one cast-iron certainty: that after every domestic disaster mother would still be there to pick up the pieces, to continue bringing up the next generation. And to continue to do it for nothing. Neither prestige nor money are awarded to her. Recently a woman wrote to *The Times* to explain her situation. She had been married for ten years and had moved about the country several times with her husband, following promotions for him, each time dislocating her own career. When she found herself at home with two small children, her husband left her for someone 'younger and richer'. Although she was returning to work—indeed she had to—her own capacity to earn had been seriously reduced because her career had had to take third place after her husband's career and her children's upbringing. She found herself in middle age in pinched circumstances, penalised for the efforts she had made for everyone else. While her husband had moved on to what was, in many senses, an enriching experience.

This is not the first time that a father has deserted his family. But, today, he can do so and not only incur the minimum of social disapproval but be 'understood'. Neither his employer nor his friends will interfere enough to say a word to restrain him. Of course, it is not always the father who goes; but if mother leaves she tends to take the children with her. Either way, it is the partner whose earning capacity and independence has never been encouraged who ends up having to earn and be independent. And father, who has been trained to support the family, finds himself cut off from them.

Responsibility without power is the doubtful prerogative of a mother in today's world. And mothers find themselves the head of their one-parent families often enough for them to begin to ask if this is really any way to run a society. Men's over-equal pay, their privileges and their quick career routes to the top have always been justified as father's share; the power of the trade unions is mobilised to see that the family provider must be paid a living wage. The rationale of past patriarchy has been that father takes the responsibility and is awarded the prestige. But father is no longer taking permanent responsibility. Very frequently he leaves the family or is discarded. Inevitably women's groups have risen up to point out that if women are so often to be treated as able to survive divorce they must be welcomed in the business and commercial world as serious contenders. Their path must be eased, not strewn with misogynist hurdles. The chauvinist trade unions who ignore women's problems must be made to look again at who today's breadwinners really are. Above all, from the state's point of view, the parent who takes on permanently the job of bringing up a stable future generation is going to be the parent who will get official support all down the line. Nations will be driven to make sure that the family can survive without father.

Yet this is not the way that many of the leaders of the Women's Liberation Movement see it. Many feminists do not really think that women should be mothers at all. Rather than cope with redesigning or re-involving father, they are tempted to abolish children. For this reason the vast majority of women listen to their message with scepticism or incomprehension. Abortion, twenty-four-hour nurseries and test-tube pregnancies are warmly discussed, while motherhood itself is referred to with some embarrassment as a sort of barbarous relic, and fatherhood is ignored. Women will never be able to take their place alongside men, it is implied, while they have those children tagging at their skirts.

Even the most eminent of women social researchers is not immune to this anti-children bias. Professor Jessie Bernard for one does not want to face the full implications of some of her own surveys. An admirer of the kind of modern marriage that is built on close equality and shared interests, she notes that children frequently cause such marriages to deteriorate. However, many of the women she interviewed,[5] while admitting that 'the effect of the children on the marriage may not be benign', nevertheless put children down as the source of their greatest satisfaction in life (38 per cent), while a very small number (8 per cent) admitted to similar satisfaction from wifehood. Referring to another survey into the lives of a group of highly educated women, Professor Bernard quotes the conclusion that 'motherhood rather than marriage seems to be the role that engages their deepest personal core.' Professor Bernard finds this 'not at all reassuring'.

One wonders why not? If this is a fact, that women find their children one of the greatest satisfactions in life, why be disturbed by it? Why not work with it? If marriage becomes more and more uncertain, the tie that remains is the tie that was first implanted by nature: that between the mother and her children. 'The irreducible and elementary social grouping is surely the mother and her children', writes anthropologist Robin Fox. 'Whatever else happens this unit has to survive for the species to survive.'[6] This is the simplest of all social ties; and perhaps it is now the tie to which we are necessarily and instinctively returning. The complexity of individual ambitions in the modern world may be making the two-parent family increasingly difficult to maintain. Among women who have already achieved the sort of personal development that others are still aiming at, it is surprising how many are divorced but highly involved with their children. Certainly a high proportion of leading women writers seem to have arrived at this position. They are hardly typical. They may be the more evolved, or simply the less adaptable; the self-developed or the self-centred. But they do suggest that life without father may be increasingly what life will be like.

But should we simply accept this? Do we just go ahead with trying to organise life more helpfully for the fatherless, or do we try to get father back? Given time and thought, it is obviously possible to replace father's material support and make the mother-headed family economically stable. But what of father's emotional contribution? Can society afford to allow men to become more and more detached from the concerns of the rising generation? Folk wisdom has generally recognised that children need a man around the house. But will mother's second or third husband do? What satisfactions do men deprive themselves of when they abandon their children, or lose custody of them? And what is the effect on society as a whole of the increasing power of mother?

To attempt to work out how agonising our loss might be if we became a society of the fatherless, and to speculate on whether this might destroy us or finally make us grow up, is the purpose of this book. We will try, in the following pages, to give father the attention he deserves. To work out his problems and satisfactions, the benefits he can confer and the problems he may create. Father has a case. But before we put it, and examine in detail the advantages for individuals and for our civilisation as a whole of persuading father to continue with a vital participation in family life, it will be easier if we first look back at father's origins.

Even today, paternity is unprovable, although it is a fact. Modern science in all its wonders still cannot tell us who the father of any particular child is. We simply know that every child had a male and a female pro-genitor. Yet even this bare fact was once unknown. There was a time when human beings were fatherless, because they could not form the idea of male involvement in reproduction. Father was not always there. He had to be found.

THREE Finding Father

Nothing about fatherhood is obvious. Patriarchy, like a visit to the ballet, is astonishing in its artificiality.

That fine edifice of social power which men have constructed over the centuries to bolster their sense of significance, to make them 'head of the family', has always been supported in defiance of the basic fact of life: nature backs mother. Witnessing the creative powers of mothers struck awe into prehistoric peoples and filled the world of early man with prayers to beneficent and fertile goddesses. But it is not simply, as the nineteenth-century lawyer Sir Henry Maine remarked, that 'paternity is a matter of inference, as opposed to maternity which is a matter of observation'. In addition to the creative reality of motherhood being so straightforward and easy to apprehend, the social tie between a mother and her offspring is so strong, so universal and so basic that it was from the very beginning of man's history the foundation of social organisation. The first examples of dependency and succour, the original lessons of mutual alliance, the first understanding that no man is an island, were gained from observing mothers and children. Because human offspring are dependent not just for weeks, as many small animals are, but for years, mother and child groups endured until they became an institution.

The original great and recurring problem of civilisation, is to find a way to include the male in this tight little group of mothers for longer than the odd bout of copulation. Incorporating men into the mother and child institution—and re-incorporating any man into a single-parent family, as many divorced mothers are finding today—is a tricky problem that demands the invention of certain social rules. What shall a man be, what shall he do? To primitive man, included in the mother-headed unit while he was a son but curiously excluded once he was grown, the problem was intense. That the mothers and children were vulnerable, particularly at certain times, offered the original clue to the perplexed male. By one of those crucial reversals of behaviour, the human male alone among the primates worked out a way not merely to outrun the female in the search for food, but to bring back to her some of what he had found; not to use his stronger muscles just to lay her and her infant low, but also to protect her. Human ingenuity and invention had as its first object the persuasion of the more powerfully built male to be helpful towards the mother-child group, rather than indifferent or aggressive. We know that wherever human life has been recorded, in whatever part of the globe, in whatever period of history, even among primitive tribes that allow us to imagine that we have glimpsed our own pre-history, adults live with children and supervise the rising generation; and mother is always one of those adults. But beyond that point it is impossible to generalise. Mothers may live alone with their children; they may live with grandmothers and aunts. Mothers and children may live in huts close to other huts containing groups of other women and children who all receive visits from the same itinerant male, as in some systems of polygyny. The woman may have as 'husband' a whole family of brothers who will all feel a common responsibility for the children. She may live with a man who is her sole sexual partner, and an affectionate companion to her children, but not understand or recognise him as her children's progenitor, turning for food, authority and protection to her brother. She may live with one sexual partner, and recognise him as the progenitor of her children and fond father as well. The modern western world is most familiar with this last form of family life. But, taking a global view, it is only one of many variations.

'The tie between a man and his wife's child can be established by any number of arrangements', writes Margaret Mead.[1]

> He may not see the child for a month after it is born; it may be attributed to him because he, among his brothers, several of whom share the same wife, performed the paternity-acknowledging ritual years ago and no other brother has performed it; he may claim it is born three

months after he had returned from a year's absence, on the
theory that it 'hurried up to see its father's face'; or in
modern rather than primitive terms, after agreeing to
artificial insemination, the mother's husband may insist 'he
really looks like me'.

The inconstant figure in family life is always the male. 'The
basic unit is the mother and child, however the mother came to
be impregnated,' writes Robin Fox, 'whether or not father can
be persuaded to stay home is another matter.'[2]

After what experiences of attack, of disease and famine men
first began to understand that survival, and even a sort of
stability, for the species could be guaranteed if they helped and
protected women and children, is beyond conjecture, but as
Margaret Mead has suggested, 'somewhere at the dawn of
human history, some social invention was made under which
males started nurturing females and their young.'[3] At this
point, the male had appreciated only that the female seemed to
find it harder to climb trees when she was on the threshold of
giving birth, and that holding an infant round her neck slowed
her down.

And he had surely noticed that she alone had the power to
produce new members of the race, and he had had a chance to
wonder exactly where he was supposed to fit into things. The
question has forever dogged the male sex. Anatomy was
destiny indeed, early man reflected bitterly, and tried to work
out ways to infiltrate himself into the system. Adding to the
female's food supply, extending her diet of herbs and roots
with the occasional meat dish seemed at least one way to
ingratiate himself. Long before males had any inkling of the
facts of physical paternity, they had managed to devise a
scheme which allowed them to become legitimate parts of the
existing structure. 'In every known human society, everywhere
in the world, the young male learns that when he grows up, one
of the things that he must do in order to be a full member of
society is to provide food for some female and her young',[4]
writes Margaret Mead, choosing her words carefully. For 'some
female' may turn out to be sister or mother rather than wife.

For a glimpse of a world in which males had formed basic
sexual alliances with females, and taken on obligations towards
women and their young without any concern as to their

contribution as biological fathers, we have to thank the Polish anthropologist Bronislaw Malinowski, who undertook three expeditions to the primitive community on the Trobriand Islands in New Guinea. His account of his experiences there, which he provocatively titled *The Sexual Life of Savages*, was a sensation among scholars and general readers alike from the day of its appearance in 1929. In meticulous and lively detail, Malinowski described a relaxed and co-operative society, where relations between the sexes were open and affectionate, where the women enjoyed equal status, where the men spent much of their time carrying the babies around in their arms, and where native wisdom and knowledge had not recognised that the male plays any part at all in the procreation of the children.

Malinowski's revelation of the life of the Trobriand islanders inspired the theorists and sexual experimenters of the 1920s; and as a supposed example of a land that succeeds without father, it has mesmerised feminists ever since. Some assumed instantly (and most were at least prepared to ask the question) that this was a phase that all human society must have experienced at some time in its past; a blissful egalitarian paradise before the artificial stimulation and growth of paternal pride.

Malinowski himself was at first able to leave a lot of the speculation to others. Instead he recounted days spent with Trobriand sorcerers who, because of their profession, knew all that there was to know in their society of human anatomy. These sorcerers acquainted Malinowski with their ideas that the discharge from both the male and female sexual organs was present solely to increase sexual pleasure; the function of the male testes was merely ornamental, he was assured. After all, a penis on its own would look a little odd.

The birth of the children was an achievement of women alone, for which they were much admired, and this was consistent with Trobriand beliefs in reincarnation. Spirit babies, waiting to be planted into females, were always present sighing in the sea-foam. A controlling spirit of some dead female relative had the task of inserting the spirit baby into the womb of her female descendant, provided that the girl was no longer a virgin. Virgins cannot conceive, the islanders conceded, because 'the way must be open'. In the Trobriand version of the beginning of the world, the original mother goddess was able to conceive after drops from a stalactite had pierced her hymen. Women were, of necessity, the first of creation. 'You see,' they explained to Malinowski, 'we are so many on the earth because many women came first. Had there been many men, we would be few'. When Malinowski challenged the ideas of the Trobriand islanders, and repeated the story that they had already had suggested to them by Christian missionaries (who were at a loss how to explain the concepts of God the Father, let alone the Immaculate Conception) that sexual intercourse with men produced conception in women, the Trobrianders offered testimony that proved to their satisfaction that this could not be so. For one thing, the island possessed a particularly ugly woman, an outcast from the group, whom no man would think of approaching; yet she had borne three children! Whereas another notorious hussy who had had intercourse with any number of men had remained childless. There the matter was dismissed. 'Only during my third expedition to New Guinea', wrote Malinowski, 'did I discover that the natives had been somewhat exasperated by having an "absurdity" preached at them, and by finding me, so "unmissionary" as a rule, engaged in the same futile argument.'[5]

Malinowski wondered, as others have wondered after him, if the Trobriand islanders were simply exercising their famous sense of humour on him; or if they did indeed know the facts of life but refused to admit them, since that would have upset their matrilineal descent and inheritance system. But the matter seemed clinched when he discovered the way the Trobrianders raised their herds of pigs. After importing a superior strain of pigs, the proud native owners immediately castrated all the males. When they were asked why, the islanders asserted, 'the female pig breeds all by itself'. In fact, as Malinowski observed, the female pigs were allowed to wander all over the island and bred with the wild boars. These same wild boars happened to be taboo animals to the people of the islands, whose flesh they were forbidden to touch. When he tried to point out how their prize pigs actually bred and what they were therefore eating, he was given to understand that he had made a remark in the worst possible taste. He was convinced that their belief in their theories was unshakeable. No men, surely, he thought, would knowingly ruin their food.

On the face of it, the beliefs of the Trobriand islanders seem to provide the foundations for a society of amiable single-parent families. It would hardly seem surprising if the men allowed the women to continue alone with the task that they had initiated alone, and bring up all the children by themselves. What makes the lesson of the Trobriand Island community so interesting, and finally so much less reassuring to the committed feminist, is that this does not happen. Quite the reverse. The islanders are so convinced of the need for male involvement in the upbringing of children that they have invented a social system that endows every child with two fathers—one the mother's sexual partner (who is the affectionate male companion to the children, though strictly an outsider in the kinship system), and the mother's brother, a more distant figure with rights of discipline, who has the responsibility of providing food and protection and who leaves his property to his sister's children. Both men take an abiding interest in the children, though neither has the possibility of formulating any feelings of pride in his 'seed'.

There is a further surprise. In the permissive climate of the Trobriands, though young girls and boys begin their sexual experience as soon and as freely as they wish, there are very few single parents. Malinowski never did find out how the islanders managed this; but he did find out why. It is socially frowned on to be an unmarried mother. The reasons the islanders give is that 'there is no father to the child, there is no man to take it in his arms.' The word 'father' used in this sense by the islanders is simply the word for 'mother's husband'. In their earthy style, they explain the very affectionate attitude of the Trobriand father as a consequence of his 'sharing in all the tender cares bestowed on the child', in helping to feed it, in ending up so often with its excrement on his hands. Affection, the Trobriand islanders accepted, is what human beings, male or female, come to feel for any child in their regular care. To the mother's brother, not involved in such daily attentions, go all the feelings of blood pride, and the obligations to provide. It is his task to fill his sister's yam house. The fathering role is split, and the children benefit from two male models, one close and affectionate, the other more remote and authoritarian.

Among the Trobriand islanders, 'the institution of the family is thus firmly established on a strong feeling of its necessity,' writes Malinowski, 'quite compatible with an absolute ignorance of its biological foundations.' The islanders were sufficiently child-centred to work out a social system that supplied the best of adult attention for every child. They were sufficiently wise to understand that paternal affection is grounded in the day-to-day care of a child, and in the man's feelings for the child's mother. If a man is with a woman during her pregnancy, when the infant is born, and takes part in caring for it, his feelings for the child will be immensely strong. The islanders knew, what modern psychologists have only in the last few years begun to perceive, that the blood tie can often be irrelevant. The bonds between adult and child depend on the mutual satisfactions of caring. 'Human paternity,' Malinowski wrote, 'which appears at first as almost completely lacking in biological foundation, can be shown to be deeply rooted in natural endowment and human need.'

If, in one civilisation, fatherhood can seem so necessary and so rewarding even when no physical tie is apparent, how much closer must it be once the facts of paternity have become known. If a man can so willingly love the children of the woman he lives with, can have such a harmonious and affectionate relationship with his son even when he does not know that he is biologically his son, what further enrichment lies in store once the blood tie is known.

Alas, it doesn't quite work out like that. The discovery of paternity does not seem to have contributed measurably to the store of human happiness. At whatever period of pre-history it occurred, the male discovery that they placed some substance in the female during intercourse which enabled her to give birth to a human being nine months later seemed to have triggered a masculine frenzy. Men began to exploit their discovery outrageously. Not content with establishing that men made a contribution, males soon asserted that theirs was the only contribution of any significance and worth, and women were designated as the mere vessel that housed the male seed. 'It seems as if father's share in parentage, once discovered, was often exaggerated', observes Edward Westermarck drily in his *History of Human Marriage*. By the time that the civilisation of the ancient Greeks, of ancient Egypt and the early Hindus are reached, the male sex had convinced itself that its members were the lords of creation.

So obsessed did men become with the majesty of their role as fathers that father religions grew up and swept mother religions aside. Many-breasted Diana, who was worshipped by the Ephesians, crumpled before the onslaught of St Paul. The sternest of the father gods, the Yahweh of the Jews, extended his dominance to Europe with the rise of Christianity. Far from recounting the origins of the world in terms of the first Great Mother, Genesis now introduced into Europe the idea of man as first upon the earth, and relegated woman to the status of one of his ribs. Only the most tenacious mediterranean instinct, repelled by the masculine Trinity, focused its affection instead on the mother of Christ, and insisted on moving the Madonna up in the scale of prestige.

Towards their children, men directed their dreams of immortality, and their ambitions as well as their love. The next generation were soon viewed as cohorts to be trained to inherit their father's wealth and skills, and taught how to continue to run it all in father's way, even after his death. Forefathers must be respected, and in some cases worshipped. This was the beginning of the conservative frame of mind. In China, before the revolution, it was the first duty of any son to marry and himself sire a son to carry on the cult of ancestor worship. Here at last was immortality.

But for women was reserved the most fatal change of heart. 'The discovery of fatherhood led to the subjection of women as the only means of securing their virtue', wrote Bertrand Russell.[6] Women, above all, had to be controlled. Their powers were such that men must see that they were not permitted to use them casually. All societies began to set rules about the circumstances in which children could be begotten. Men wanted to become fathers, so they had to become husbands. Women, as breeding vessels, had to be given or awarded to other men. And so the complexities of marriage and the patrilineal family began to evolve.

The male fervour for guaranteed, legitimate offspring made life miserably constrained for women throughout most of history. Energy, expression and will, which could be admired in sons, simply caused anxiety in daughters. Curiosity and intelligence and the development of a strong personality were frowned upon, as signs that a woman might be astute enough to evade constant male supervision. A woman's honour came to

When he grows up he will feel obliged for some years, as his mother has impressed on him, to contribute to her household and send her money even if he goes far away to work (even as far as Britain). The female that the Jamaican male learns to provide for is his mother. His devotion to her is fundamental and extends well into adult life; possibly it does not help him to develop new and permanent loyalties to a sexual mate. His reactions may be chilly indeed towards the man who, as Jamaican writer George Lamming expressed it, 'had only fathered the idea of me and left me the sole liability of my mother who really fathered me.'

In evaluating the current family problems of western societies, and in assessing the effects of the trauma of divorce and separation on children and the bitterness of disillusion brought to adults, the question keeps recurring that possibly mothers should be encouraged to assume all the responsibility for family life from the beginning, since this is what they will find themselves doing in the end. Why not let mother start out alone, or with a partner who is recognised as an impermanent figure? Some argue that this could make for a more fluid but consistent family life. The worst hurts of divorce and separation would be avoided; the departing male would merely be fulfilling his expected role. Society, it is suggested, might find it cheaper and easier to finance mothers from the word go, rather than spend so much on medical and social workers to pick up the pieces once marriages break up. The state could organise itself more efficiently to back the figure nature backs, mother. Society would have no need to bully father into remaining in his customary responsible place.

But the example of Jamaican family life suggests why such theories may be mere delusion. It is hard to escape the conclusion that adult males who are not in some way induced to accept the domestic yoke end up a nuisance to themselves, to their women and their children. The men of the Trobriand Islands give the impression of possessing a key to an effective and stable life that many Jamaican men have apparently mislaid. That mothers can, even in discouraging economic conditions like those of Jamaica, take on the whole burden with merely part-time help from grandmothers, lovers and growing children seems to be true. But once this is allowed to become a repeated and accepted pattern, very real social problems are created and must be recognised. By allowing the mother role to involve too much responsibility, the father role is then designed to encourage irresponsibility. Boys grow up to understand that men are the frivolous sex. Men return to their prehistoric status where they belong to society as sons, but once adult are disconnected and apart. Without the role of fatherhood, men have no motive to join the community as responsible citizens, to use their talents in socially constructive ways, to restrain their aggression for the common good, to contribute to the rising generation. Once father departs, there is no one to teach the burdens and benefits of fatherhood to his son. Marriage begets marriage; and divorce, non-marriage and fatherlessness beget their like.

Our western society has already pushed far along this road of elevating mother and increasing her responsibilities, and allowing the father role to fall into decline. As we have already seen, father's basic and primitive role—that of provider and protector—has today dwindled into lesser significance. Mother is helping to pay the food bill, and if threatened or attacked she calls the police. Governments have begun to assume that if they want to fortify the next generation, the most direct way to do it is to help the mothers. Against all earlier patriarchal habits of mind and of administration, the Family Allowance payment for children, when it was first introduced in Britain after World War II, was paid to mothers. A recent threat to change this, and to lump allowance together with other tax remissions payable to fathers 'for administrative convenience', stirred up an animated and successful grass-roots campaign among women which was able to convince the government that money granted to mothers finds its way directly to the children, while money paid to fathers may not.

Father has been further nudged aside by the dominant trends of modern psychology. Psychology from the beginning sliced through the artificial, carefully constructed ties of patriarchy to reveal the emotional reality that was always at the base of the family; the mother and child bond. Like many a great truth, this discovery has proved to be ambiguous in its social consequences.

As much as any school of medieval painting, modern psychology has obsessively concerned itself with 'the mother-child dyad'. The relationship of the mother and her child has become the most sacred, the most important, the most studied in the whole book. Psychology has re-created the Madonna. It is not simply accepted today that mother feeds, cleans and takes the baby for a walk; any Victorian would have known that without some woman's physical care an infant would not survive. Our century has shown scientifically and exhaustively that, without a mother's love and interest, the child will not grow emotionally and intellectually. It is her maternal passion that warms an infant to the capacity to feel affections himself; it is her interest that gives him a sense of his own worth; her ingenuity that awakes his creativity, her joie de vivre that makes him eager to tackle life. Because of psychology's emphasis on the deeply-rooted link between mother and child and its importance in producing a sane future generation, countless researchers have studied the relationship in infinite detail. We now know, for example, that if a mother leaves a child between the ages of 1½ and 2½ for more than twenty-four hours, that child starts to regress. We have no idea what happens if that same child's father goes off on a business trip and leaves him for two whole months.

'What is believed to be essential for mental health is that an infant and young child should experience a warm, intimate and continuous relationship with his mother in which both find satisfaction and enjoyment'—the words of John Bowlby, whose studies of maternal deprivation for the World Health Organisation in 1951,[11] translated and reprinted again and again, have done more than anything to convince an entire generation of government officials and mothers that this is where planning for the future really starts. But in later pages of the same work, Bowlby's colleague Mary Ainsworth lets drop a footnote which recognises apologetically, 'while maternal deprivation has preoccupied investigators for the past thirty years, paternal deprivation has received scant attention.'

And today, twenty-five years further on, this is still the case. Mother still occupies the centre of the stage. If the children turn out successfully, she is bathed in glory. If they become schizophrenic, then she is to blame. Either way, no one suspects that father may have had a hand in it. Many feminists have cried 'foul' at this renewing of the cult of the mother goddess and have attacked psychologists for producing still one more male rationale to keep women in the nursery and out of the competitive world of men. One of the paradoxes of modern living certainly seems to be that the more well-read the mother, the more time she spends with her pre-school child. But feminists frequently fail to see that it is the psychologists who have written 'finis' to Victorian patriarchy. Under the influence of the psychologists, legislators and judges have come to feel that if we want to avoid rearing antisocial and unstable individuals, the relationship of the younger generation and their mothers must be protected.

The needs of mothers are currently being promoted not just by pressure groups of one-parent families, nor by revolutionaries who are delighted to toll the bell for the decline and fall of the nuclear family. A campaign to secure a state pension for all one-parent families now has official support. The Report of the Committee on One-Parent Families, published after four and a half years of research and deliberation by Sir Morris Finer and his colleagues, came to the conclusion that for many reasons divorce and separation will be increasingly with us, that many one-parent families will continue to be the result, and that the children of these families will suffer social disabilities which will make them ill-educated, under-achieving citizens that a modern nation can do without. Its suggestion is that a state pension for one-parent families is the only answer. We are recommended to plan for life without father.

The writing on the wall is now sufficiently legible for men to begin to query their situation. The tip of the iceberg is revealed as some of the most hard-pressed divorced fathers organise and make their voices heard. 'Families Need Fathers' is the name and war-cry of a group of British husbands who since divorce find it increasingly impossible ever to meet their children, let alone work out how to remain important to them. In campaigning to get the law on 'access' strengthened, these fathers are also challenging the stereotype of the ever-loving mother, to which they think the official world is now in thrall, and trying to focus the paternal role more sharply. In France, the initials DIDHEM cloak the similar efforts of the society *Défense des Intérêts des Divorcés hommes et leurs Infants mineurs.* Germany, Denmark, and other European countries are seeing similar groups spring up. And in the United States, Boston's 'Fathers United for Equal Justice' is campaigning to get the possibility of an ever-loving father accepted, and to assert that he has some rights to see and care for his children.

The father role has reached crisis point. Father's lessening intervention in the family, if too readily accepted, could allow him to disappear altogether. The shift in responsibility and power between the sexes, inside the family and in society at large, the focus on the changing opportunities of women, has not been paralleled by any really hard thought on the possibilities ahead for men. Under conditions of sufficient stress, as we know, after wars and famines, the tradition which teaches men how to be fathers to the next generation can break down. Possibly the present revolution in values faces men with just such a critical period and they may be finding that the institution of fatherhood is becoming unworkable. Current changes are too many and too fast for men to know what is required of them in their family role. They no longer feel certain that they are needed; they have few ideas as to what they are needed for.

Father may have only two alternatives; to redefine and reinvent his role or to abandon it. It seems to be in the best interests of men, women and children to help to find a formula that keeps father in the family. By abandoning merely the excesses of the past, men may find themselves with a less limited part to play in the family.

Father may now be able to look forward to a period that is not merely a postscript to the patriarchal past. In parting with their traditional dominance, men may be arriving at the point where they can enjoy their children naturally for the first time in centuries. At all events, fatherhood must not be allowed to dwindle away without discussion or awareness of what is happening. We must attempt to assess the case for father.

ɪOUR The Case for Father: Fathers and Sons

To the question 'what is father for?', many families would answer in one word: money. Millions still maintain their whole way of life, the ownership of their house and car, the clothes they wear and the holidays they enjoy on the income of one individual, the husband and father. Such families' whole standard of living reflects father's competence as a provider. Many thousands of other women and children also see father primarily as a provider, because they are not provided for. They are bitterly aware that the reason they do not enjoy many things that others have is that no man makes it his job to see that they get them.

Although the world we live in is fast changing shape, enough of the old patriarchal structure remains for the fatherless still to be at sore material disadvantage. The fatherless child is worse housed, worse fed, worse clothed, worse educated and worse supervised than the child who knows his father is around and taking an interest in the family. While making do without father, such children also see less of mother than others do; she has to be out and about, not only earning the family income but dealing with every detail of their lives from getting the new car licence to hiring the camping equipment for the rare weekend in the country. So monotonously do the fatherless turn up in the poverty and social deprivation statistics that psychologists and social workers attempting to come to grips with and define the specific characteristics of fatherlessness find themselves bogged down among the basic questions of survival that the poor have always had to face. Experts who have tried to write about the fatherless come up against the same problem. As Margaret Wynn was forced to confess at the beginning of her book *Fatherless Families*, 'Many of the consequences of fatherlessness discussed in this study are primarily the consequences of poverty.' To lose his father is the worst bit of bad luck, from the material point of view, that can happen to a child today. It is possible to insure against father dying, which was the chief misfortune of the last century. But there is as yet no way to insure against divorce or separation, which is the disaster that removes father today.

It may seem that if father is still so crucially important in terms of material support no more need be said. Of course he has a case, an economic one, and that is an end of the matter. But father's position as a provider is not an unqualified source of strength. In fact, quite the reverse. Because he looms so large as a source of income, he has been allowed to loom so small as a person. Because he generally has been the provider, he has come to be looked on as nothing more. He has been assigned the part of financial backer of the family performance, while mother has taken the starring role.

Father's conventional providing role has been the cause of his physical separation from his family, and the source of much expert dismissal of his personal contribution to family life. A man's total involvement in the competitive world of business has been motivated and approved of as central to his providing role, and has left him with no time for any other. Many years ago Geoffrey Gorer epitomised the United States as 'the Motherland' and accused American men of being 'so wrapped up in the pursuit of success that they largely abdicate control over their children's upbringing to their wives.' Father's role, in the United States, Gorer decided was 'vestigial'. No better assumptions about father's usefulness exist in Britain. In the immediate post-war period reforms of British orphanages into small cottage homes were organised under resident *house-mothers* to achieve 'normal family life' for the children. Since the bills were paid by the state, no one seemed to think a house-father might be needed at all. And John Bowlby, while superbly sensitive to all the subtleties of the mother-child relationship, has been able to write that the father 'is of no direct importance to the young child, but is of indirect value as an economic support and in his emotional support of the mother.'

Bowlby's peculiar blindness to father's existence as a person and his dominance of his field has led to a generation of research that has studiously avoided noticing anything much in family relationship except the ties between mother and children. Only in recent years have some expert voices been raised in protest. Michael Rutter, the child psychiatrist, complains, 'there are no studies of the short-term effects of paternal absence and the influence of the father has been greatly neglected.'[1]

By awarding father the blank role of a mere signer of cheques we have also made him look replaceable. After all, does it matter who signs the cheques, so long as the bank balance is healthy? Providing is something that even those outside the family can do. Society has only to organise another system of child endowment to dispense with father altogether. This may sound a revolutionary idea but in fact it has already been acted on. It is basic to the very different ways that we currently try to solve the problems of one-parent families. If the family is motherless, for any reason, the state and the local community will try to find another *person* who can step into mother's place. Father can, and is even expected to, advertise for a housekeeper and mother-substitute. But if a family is fatherless for any reason, everyone assumes that mother can cope with all the personal problems on her own. All that is sought is an alternative source of income. 'If I tried to advertise for a "father-substitute", my friends and neighbours would think that I was trying to solve my sexual problems, not to do the children a bit of good', says one lone mother.

So father's case, the importance of father as part of the human family, has to be argued outside the providing role. Providing is slippery, replaceable territory, and already, in the majority of families, shared between both parents. The unique contribution of father, his plea to be taken seriously in the future of the human family, has to be calculated in personal terms. In what ways does he affect the development of his children; what are the things that noticeably go right if he does a good job of fathering, what are the things that go wrong if he does not? And what is good fathering anyway?

For every fifty psychologists working on various aspects of mother-child relationships, there has been one, in more recent years, willing to turn some attention to the mysteries of what can happen between father and child. The theories put forward, the research done, though small in quantity, is thick with contradictions. The method of the investigators often leaves much to be desired; a number of surveys have been carried out solely by asking mothers! And some of the questions asked have been so imbued with sexual politics that the results are meaningless. Even so, there are a few general conclusions to be drawn. Some of them would not surprise any family that had always assumed that the smile the baby gave to his father when he arrived home meant something. Yet others do provide new food for thought.

It takes very little imagination to recognise that a man's influence over the life of his child can start long before the fact of birth. The excitement and affection, or lack of both, at the time of conception, the thoughts and actions of the father on hearing of the pregnancy, all influence the mother's attitude to her coming child. Adoption agencies, who deal regularly with unmarried mothers in the agonising debate of whether to keep their child or relinquish it for adoption, testify that one of the crucial factors which influence the final decision is the mother's view of how significant or meaningless was her affair with the father. Inside marriage also, the atmosphere between the parents during the wife's pregnancy, the intensity of anticipation of the child's birth by both parents, or the wife's self-absorption in the face of her husband's lack of interest, all have their effect on the ease and strength that both parents have to find to deal with the squalling infant once it arrives.

'I remember my husband's reaction when I told him about my first pregnancy,' says one wife. 'Before he could check himself he said, "how on earth did you let that happen?" I have never had any confidence in his interest in the children from that moment.'

Once the child is born, the conventional view has been that mother will get on with the job of infant-rearing, and that, apart from the occasional encouraging pat for her, father has nothing much to do until the children are vocal, energetic and defiant teenagers who may need to be brought to heel. However, the merest beginning of research into family relationships in these early years has been enough to blow such a view sky-high. Perhaps the most significant point that has emerged is that if father allows himself to be kept aside as unimportant to the very young child, he may have set the pattern to remain unimportant to that child for ever after.

Psychologists are chary of taking over whole into the study of human development present knowledge of how animals are 'imprinted' with bonds and patterns of behaviour at crucial periods of their growth. But knowledge of how small goslings can learn to follow the mother goose at certain stages of their development, and how if they miss out on the necessary teaching at that time, they will fail for ever more to get the point, has opened up a number of questions about 'imprinting' in human relationships. Psychologists have begun to ask whether there is a critical period in which not only can the small child learn to become attached to his parents, including father, but father can also be stimulated into close feelings for the child. *Imprinting, if it works, works both ways.* At the moment, though nothing is proved, the presumption is that something very like imprinting does take place, that it takes place early, certainly within the first three years of a child's life, and that if this period is missed, neither the child nor the father will be as receptive to the same sort of experience later.

Families who have endured war-time separations are painfully aware that this can be so. Sam Cornwall's eldest son was born while he was away on a scientific expedition, and he did not see the boy until he was two and a half years old. He felt nothing but a strange repulsion at the first sight of his child. The feelings were mutual. Young Daniel howled with terror and jealousy at this huge stranger who suddenly arrived to claim so much of his mother's attention; it was much worse than the arrival of a baby brother because this man obviously had senior status. Daniel's father found it difficult to be encouraging or firm with the boy. Yet his other two children, who arrived in later years, whose birth he witnessed and whose early weeks he watched, never seemed a problem to him. For years, Daniel got the blame for the awkwardness in their relationship. 'I've never felt at ease with that boy,' Sam always said critically, 'but the others are so straightforward.'

Father's part after the infant years in teaching the children to become fully human obviously starts by just being there, giving them enough time to seize on the fact that men exist as well as women, that interesting and helpful, satisfying and violent feelings can exist between father and mother, as well as father and son, mother and son, father and daughter and mother and daughter. To be introduced to the rich emotional possibilities of life, a growing child needs to see some of it in action.

Most of all, children of both sexes get a chance to see how men and women get along together as adults. They observe that father makes more noise, but does not always win the arguments. That mother is good at tactical weeping, and that sometimes this wins her the day. They observe the compliments and hidden threats, the good-will and the resentments in the life of any married couple. From whom does a young boy learn how to be a confident husband, if not from the first husband he saw in action—his father?

Children who live without a father are liable to have as much concrete knowledge of how men behave as they have a realistic picture of dragons and ghosts and space monsters, or any of the other creatures that people their imagination. Researchers have observed young boys and girls playing with male and female dolls, and formed the opinion that the fatherless children used the male dolls in their games in remarkably mild and unlifelike ways. Their father-dolls were just too nice. The children who had first-hand knowledge of how father could behave let their dolls kick up a fuss from time to time.

Very little research work has been done on father; and even less on step-father. How different step-father's influence might be can at the moment only be guessed at. Research has so far presumed that no other male but father is involved intensely enough, or permanently enough, in the family emotional crucible. A man who is interested only in mother, or eager only to be a friend to the children, or who is able to be any of these things only for a few years at a time, cannot supply the same range of feelings and understandings. As one divorced father comments, 'any other male except father is only too likely to be a bird of passage.'

Because of father's presence in the family, the whole complicated process known as 'father-identification' can begin to take place. Though psychologists have confessed that identification is not a very precise term and 'it is difficult to say just what it means', it seems to come down to a child appreciating the existence of a significant adult, wanting to be like him, being willing to learn from him and wanting to be accepted by him as significant in turn. This is obviously something that happens to an immeasurable extent with most mothers. If father is around enough, and if mother is also able to encourage it, it happens with him as well. But because he is not mother, the children are offered a different personality to learn from, and a different sex to join or subtly seduce. The child is also offered a different 'wavelength' to tune in to. Psychiatrist Robert Andry considers this to be one of the most important choices that the two-parent family offers to any child. 'A quiet and lethargic baby may find a special bond with a quiet and lethargic father rather than with a bouncy extrovert mother. There are so many variables in the ways that people relate to each other in the family'.

From the chance to observe and learn from the way father and mother cope with each other and the world the children can take in very early in life an appreciation of social and sexual roles that is thought to be crucial for the boy and also important for the girl. Even those who are most suspicious of the indoctrination of small children into rigid ways of behaving and rigid expectations of what it means to be masculine or feminine will probably be willing to ask whether the fatherless son and the motherless daughter may not be, in very special ways, deprived.

The importance of the parent of the same sex in the development of any child is one of the most basic of family strands. Girls tend to be lucky, since the model they need to give them daily reassurance that life can be lived is generally on hand demonstrating the fact. A boy has the harder task of understanding that the parent who is in charge of him for most hours of the day, the teacher who controls and encourages him in his first ventures outside the world of the family, belong to the sex that he is not expected to join. If his father is not around to illustrate that men have their own tasks—often maybe very similar tasks to women but masculine because they are doing them their own way—their own satisfactions, and their ways of coping with the powerful female sex, the boy may grow into an uncertain man who believes that there are only two ways of dealing with women: you either lick 'em or join 'em. Living with women, enjoying their difference without feeling the need to deal with them either way, is one of the lessons a boy is hoped to be able to learn at his father's knee.

Exactly how father wins over his sons so that they are willing to learn from him, to identify with him, is the subject of great contention. Freud, in his Oedipus theory, saw the three-year-old boy loving and wanting to possess his mother exclusively, and reacting to father first in jealous rage and fear as a rival. Fears of his father as the stronger suitor to mother are gradually resolved in the child as he accepts that, although he is not going to win this woman, he can join the winning side and be like father, so that he will gain another woman some day. Though the child's emotional turmoil is viewed by Freud as highly complex, it is basically fear of the big father that wins his son to his side.

Since such frightening fathers are now in rather short supply, however, the motive force of fear has obviously weakened. What seems to count much more is that a warm and loving father encourages the feeling in his son that he will continue in the path that father has forged, and that through affection for his father, not fear, reproduce in himself 'bits of the beloved parent'.

Possibly, the child's willingness to identify with the parent of his own sex depends on his envy and admiration for the special rewards that this parent enjoys. Father has mainly, therefore, to indicate to his son the status advantages of growing up like him. (It seems at the moment that a lot of girls have perceived the status disadvantages of their mother's position and vowed not to grow up like her.) But the small boy can want to identify with the role of his father, in so far as he sees him as a master of the environment. From any and from all of these theories, one or all of which may bear some relation to reality, it is obvious that if father is not there, either in body or in spirit, the boy's development becomes more problematical. And that once again it is the early years that count.

The support and enrichment of a son's development involves, as anyone can imagine, a great deal more than father's mere presence. The father's own character, the extent to which he has made a success of his own personal life, plus his ability to pass these intangibles on through his easy affection with his son, are at the root of his son's ready acceptance of being male. His son learns about masculinity from father. 'It is the total relationship that counts', sums up University of Rhode Island psychologist Henry B. Biller.[2]

Many fathers have masculine interests and are masculine in

their peer and working relationships but are very ineffectual in their interactions with their wives and children. The stereotype of the masculine, hard-working father whose primary activity at home is lying on the couch watching television, or sleeping, is an all too accurate description of many fathers. If the boy's father is not consistently involved in family functioning it is much harder for his son to learn to be appropriately assertive, aggressive and independent.

There seem to be definite differences in development between boys who grow up with a father and boys who do not. But whether father is present or absent is not the most crucial dividing line. It is what kind of a father he is when he is there that is really important. Quality is what counts.

The delicate territory of measuring 'masculinity' is ground where psychologists have not feared to tread. And whatever the questions raised, some of the tests they have devised cast an interesting light on how an involved father does influence the way his son grows. A maths versus verbal ability score has been constructed that generally shows boys scoring higher on the maths and analytical tests and girls scoring highest on the verbal and communications skills so consistently that the analytical maths mind can be associated with 'masculinity', and verbal skill with 'femininity'. By feeding the maths versus verbal ability tests to some middle-class high school boys in the United States who had experienced a period *before the age of five* of living without their fathers (those fathers were then involved in World War II), psychologist Lyn Carlsmith discovered that these boys showed a mental pattern of high verbal score that was frequently the same as the female pattern. What is more, Carlsmith wrote when publishing her findings in the *Harvard Educational Review*, 'the relative superiority of verbal to math aptitudes increases steadily the longer the father is absent and the younger the child when the father left.' Missing father for a few years early in life has marked the mental patterns and aptitudes of these boys over a decade later. Even though their fathers did return. Would they have been affected even more if father had stayed away for the rest of their lives? And in what other areas of living, impossible to measure but important to their enjoyment and management of their lives, may they turn out to be specially endowed or specially lacking?

Mental aptitude is not the only aspect of development that seems to be decided early in life and decisively influenced by relations with both parents. Perhaps most vital for any individual's later happiness is the whole question of understanding and accepting which sex he or she belongs to. Research into the rare cases of transexuals who have never settled psychologically into the same sex as the physical body they were born with points to the first two or three years of life as being the time in which individuals perceive themselves as male or female, and indicates that such perceptions are very difficult indeed to shift after that time. A recent public witness to this is James/Jan Morris, who relates in her account of her sex change, *Conundrum*, that the conviction first came at the age of three, when sitting under the family piano, that although he had been christened James and inhabited a boy's body, he was really a girl.

It is in this early period that the normal boy has to realise and accept that he will grow up to be like father, not like mother; that having accepted a view of himself as masculine, he effectively carries this through in his behaviour with adults and other children; and that he chooses to abide by the main social rules about what is appropriate behaviour for his sex.

In all of these aspects of settling into his sexual role a young boy can be helped by the presence of an involved father and confused and hindered by an absent or ineffectual one. But his problems are not perhaps as acute as some have tried to claim. If the fatherless boy always found it impossible to act like a male in any sense, we would all have noticed it with our own eyes by now. Experiments to test sexual differences between the fathered and unfathered arouse some scepticism, anyway. In fact, by inviting young children to complete drawings of male and female figures, to answer questions about how they might behave in certain situations and to pick out favourite toys and games, researchers have come to the conclusion that there are not many marked differences in the field of general manners and behaviour between boys who are adequately fathered and those who are not. Boys obviously learn how to behave like boys from many people outside the home, from grandfather, uncles and particularly from other children. Mother herself tries to bring up her son to be manly, despite her handicaps. Very few women, after all, want their boys to be effeminate.

But in the internal matter of self-perception, of feeling male, there appears to be an area of uncertainty in boys who have not experienced fathering. And psychologists warn that a young boy who is uncertain about his sexuality can find pressures to assume a masculine role acutely uncomfortable. Because he cannot himself 'feel' secure in his masculine attitudes, he is easily convinced by others of his own age group, who may be equally confused, that to become masculine he must become aggressive and even violent. The street-corner gang in a deprived neighbourhood, where perhaps up to 50 per cent of the boys are without father, or have a father who can give little instruction in how to deal effectively with the world, works out its own rules as to what is tough and manly, and its guidelines can often be vicious and infantile. That such a group of adolescent boys can easily erupt into the violence of murder and rape, that contempt for the older and weaker becomes the only law, has been illustrated with some glamour in the film of Anthony Burgess's *Clockwork Orange*. A total and fearful rejection of everything female and feminine is usually one of the cornerstones of such a gang. But under the heading of 'feminine' may be rejected even the most basic rules of civilisation and the whole of education, since the disciplines of both home and school, as they have known them, were enforced by women.

Thriller-writer Ian Fleming in many ways epitomises the uncertain fatherless boy, just as his creation, the ruthless secret service agent James Bond, sums up the fantasies of the fatherless. Fleming's father was killed in World War I, and at Eton Ian was always overshadowed by his elder brother Peter, a brilliant scholar and athlete. With a 'dead hero' father, a formidable mother and a brilliant brother, Ian Fleming grew up as a hero-worshipper, very unable to believe in his own talents. 'Ian Fleming's early life', suggests psychologist Anthony Storr,[3] 'is a catalogue of disappointment and failure of a kind characteristic of boys who have been unable to identify with a real father, and who consequently develop little confidence in their own abilities, however considerable these abilities may be in reality'. The James Bond books, full of sadism, contempt for women disguised by a collector's catalogue of their attractions, and frequent plots to castrate the hero, can engross and amuse a psychiatrist as well as a thriller addict.

It is hardly surprising that father's part in getting his sons to feel the pride and responsibility inherent in being boys is important. Traditionally father has been the one to emphasise sex differences in the family, to encourage his son to keep his cool and maintain 'a stiff upper lip', while permitting his daughter to have a good cry; to make his son work hard and look forward to years of achievement while letting his daughter feel that being good and sweet is enough. Psychologists and sociologists agree that father is supposed to be the chief transmitter of culturally-based conceptions of masculinity and femininity. Those conceptions are quite rightly at the present time under fierce attack, and father is directly in the firing line. Feminist critics view father with understandable distaste, and accuse him of training his sons to assume the mantle of male dominance. But there is a more generous way of interpreting father's influence. What if father needs to be there in some degree to ensure that his sons have at least a fighting chance in the battle of the sexes? Boys may need father's backing before they can confidently lay claim to their own future as males.

Though a boy seems to need his father most in the years before five, the rest of his childhood also contributes to the man he ultimately becomes. And folk wisdom has always to some extent recognised this. Growing up alongside a father who talks to him, takes a constant interest in him, makes decisions that his son is aware of, sets some limits to what his son may or may not do, gets his son to work with him on jobs and play with him in sports, enriches and smooths the transition from young child to adolescent. If his father knows how to praise and encourage rather than criticise and undermine, he will learn all the faster. The 'heavy father', pompous and authoritarian, seems simply to put his son off.

To a man like James Herriot, author of *All Creatures Great and Small*, an account of his life as a vet in the Yorkshire Dales, fathering came as naturally as responding to the needs of animals. From the time that they could stand up, Herriot's small son and daughter accompanied their father on his rounds. Herriot himself recounts:

both the children used to come out in the car with me all the

time once they were two years old. They would put their big
boots on and off we'd go. My children would open the gates
and get my bottles out of the boot. They knew every one of
them. When my daughter had to go to school when she was
five, she was worried how I'd manage without her. 'Never
mind, Dad,' she said, 'I'll be with you on Saturdays.'

After an entire childhood of living and helping so closely
alongside their father, Herriot's son grew up to be a vet also,
and his daughter became a doctor; the son is now a partner in
his father's practice.

If father is not there in the years after five, a number of
different problems can arrive for his son. Father's absence may
well set up intellectual hurdles. Sorting out why some children
persistently underachieve and never learn to work to their
fullest capabilities, while others possess the stamina and
concentration to exploit to the full their quite modest talents,
is a field of research which is both fascinating in personal terms
and significant in its potential effect on social planning. The
parents' attitude is crucial in determining a child's educational
prowess, and there is growing evidence that a father can pass on
to his son the will to succeed academically or the lack of nerve
that leads to failure. Educational performance is more easily
investigated than sexual development, and yields more
concrete and reliable findings. One enquiry which con-
centrated on underachieving primary schoolboys discovered
that the fathers of these boys were men who considered
themselves inadequate and doomed to failure, and that the sons
were offered no example of how to tackle life confidently. The
mothers in these families also saw the fathers as incompetent
figures. The boys had accepted their only inheritance—dismay.

Even more interesting was a check into the academic
performance of American third-grade boys. Henry Biller and a
colleague matched the boys for social class, IQ, age and number
of brothers and sisters, but divided them into four groups;
those who had absent fathers before they were five years old,
those who had absent fathers after they were five, those who
had fathers who gave them only about six hours of their time a
week and those who had fathers who gave them more than two
hours of their attention per day. The findings were clear. The
boys who saw a great deal of their fathers each day easily came

out top; those who had missed fathering in their earliest years were generally the most severe underachievers. The other partially deprived children seldom found it easy to make the grade.

An influence that is only too easy to dismiss as simply old patriarchs' tales shows up therefore as very real in a scrupulous modern study. If the father is a capable man, if he has a good, affectionate relationship with his son, and if they are able to spend plenty of time together, the boy can be given the sort of start in life that every boy needs. And in so far as father is playing a traditional role, he passes on traditional abilities. His son is prodded into 'masculine' aptitudes (that is high on maths and low on verbal skills) by something more subtle than simply spending time in an adult male's company.

For the curious fact is that the 'masculine' mentality may not develop in boys who are looked after by lone fathers, men who spend their days in the intense relationships with their children that is more usually confined to mothers. It seems to be necessary for a father to be sufficiently detached from the details of his children's day for him to preserve some object- ivity and extra clarity, but involved enough for him to pass on the benefits of this particular cast of mind. The subtle influences of the parent's role as well as his sex is suggested by surveys of orphans, all boys, who received full-time care from male nurses; they registered in aptitude tests as nearer the female norm than the male. Presumably, this happens because the male nurse who is occupied in full-time care ends up 'mothering', that is assuming the intense traditional female role, and so becomes in some way incapable of passing on and encouraging in a boy the traditional 'masculine' outlook and abilities. The 'masculine' mind may be formed only by coming into contact with a mind that is already that way.

The speculations aroused are endless. If it is the role, and the kind of mind that role produces, that has so much influence on the child, can a sufficiently detached mother pass on some of the same intellectual inheritance? And could not father create such a 'masculine' mind in either his sons or his daughters? We may well be using unnecessary terms.

A lone, intelligent mother can obviously stimulate her son's intelligence anyway, even if she is more likely to unearth in him a talent as a writer rather than a talent as an engineer. That

Leonardo da Vinci's earliest years were spent in a one-parent family with a mother who managed to inspire both such talents, and plenty more, in her son, bears witness that the situation is not as straightforward as paternalists may wish to suggest. What a child needs is someone to take an interest in his school work. There may be advantages for him if that someone is a much-loved father; there may be just as many if that someone is a very close mother. Observing the differences between success and failure in a New York ghetto school, Bernard Mackler concluded: 'having a father in the home does not insure success, nor does his absence insure failure. What is common to most successful children is an adult, usually mother, whose interest in the child and his education . . . is keenly sensed by the child.'[4]

In fact the whole question of father's influence on his son's intelligence is seen from a slightly different angle if it is shifted through the social classes. In lower-class families, where it is unfortunately likely that the man still has a monopoly on any skill going, if father is not there his son suffers by being brought up by a mother who is harassed and ignorant, rather than simply by a mother. In middle-class families, if father departs, the effects on his son's intelligence may be much less marked. Growing up in an intense emotional situation with an intelligent mother may be dangerous in terms of a boy's sexual development (Leonardo, we remember, was homosexual), but often in the past this has proved to be the forcing-house of genius. Looking at today's college population it has been shown that a bright lone mother, widowed or divorced, is often the figure behind a successful male student—but that his abilities do tend to be literary rather than mathematical.

Mother may well be able to offer an alternative form of intellectual guidance to her son, albeit with emotional strings attached, but there are strong arguments to suggest that father plays an essential part in a boy's character development, in teaching his son the disciplines of self and of society. It seems partly to be that if boys perceive the rules and regulations of life as coming entirely from women, from mothers and from teachers who are usually women—they find it hard in adolescence not to kick aside all social restraints at the same time that they are trying to assert themselves as males. If father however is pointing out the rules and the reasons for them, they are not offered the same easy opportunity to see all rule-observance as effeminate.

For Sigmund Freud, father is the architect of the three-tier structure of the human personality. If we are all, as he suggested, divided into three parts, a primitive instinctive id, a rational essential ego, and a disciplining conscience or super-ego, that last civilising part is largely constructed in the child by his father. It is father, according to Freud, who teaches his children what is forbidden, what is considered wicked, what they must not do; in learning these lessons, the child develops a capacity for guilt, for accepting blame and for taking father's standards into his own personality in the form of 'conscience'. Simultaneously, it is father who teaches what are the highest ideals, the values a child should live by. This all sounds very Victorian to us, and it can be dismissed as belonging more to the Viennese bourgeoisie of Freud's own day than to any modern family. We are only too aware that mother's work and effort, mother's involvement in family and wider social morality, is as deep as father's. However, Freud did have one crucial point to make about father's fitness to be the chief disciplinarian that is dependent not on his status but on masculine emotional reactions. Father is by nature less indulgent to his children. According to classical Freudian theory, father is uniquely equipped to make sure these lessons are learnt by his children, because he offers them a prize: his attention and esteem. Father's is love that must be won.

The classic view of the difference between an ideal father's love for his children and a mother's love has been defined with great lucidity by Erich Fromm:[5] 'Motherly love by its nature is unconditional. Mother loves the newborn infant because it is her child, not because the child has fulfilled any specific condition, or lived up to any specific expectation.' So delicious is it to be loved for oneself, and not because one has done anything to deserve it, that all adults hunger for the same kind of passion for the rest of their lives. But such indulgent love, says Fromm, although it gives us the first will to live, implies no moral law. The greatest criminals can be produced by a mother who allows her sons to feel that they can do no wrong. Father's love, he says, is quite different. 'Fatherly love is conditional love. Its principle is "I love you *because* you fulfill my expectations, because you do your duty, because you are like me." It is a love that can be won, by effort, by trying to understand the rules and by learning how to live within them.'

Most parents, however, probably try to be 'mother' and 'father' at the same time. Mothers spend long hours of their day restraining their children from pushing the baby over in a fit of jealous rage, or trying out their new-found skill with scissors on the kitchen curtains. They get used to conveying to their children the subtle message, 'I love you, but I don't always like what you do.' And fathers are capable of loving and admiring their sons, not just for playing by the rules, but for succeeding in the invention of new rules entirely. Many a father has managed to register both disappointment that his son has not made the football team like he did, and delight in that same son's scholastic success that may exceed anything father was ever capable of. Love and instruction can, and indeed must, go together; but some children may find it easier in their own minds to feel: 'Mother will comfort me, and father will tell me off.'

Once again, this is difficult territory to poke about in and try to measure. Yet boys without fathers have been reported as lacking in self-esteem and initiative, as over-aggressive, as more impulsive, and generally less able to follow the rules of society. The conclusion has been that if a boy hasn't learnt how to get along with a father, he may always find it difficult to cope with male figures in authority such as the headmaster, the boss, the bank manager and the policeman.

The rash of juvenile delinquency that most countries in the west are currently experiencing has been blamed on many factors in our present society: on the breakdown of traditional religious beliefs and the change in social values, on violent examples on television, on our smash-and-grab capitalist system, on emotional maladjustment following separation from mother in childhood, on a background of poverty and social deprivation, on the lack of interest on the part of both parents in spending time with their children and their abandonment to the sheep-like direction of their peer group from nursery school to teenage gang. But among the many possible ways of accounting for the large numbers of young people who run foul of the law is the fact noted by social workers and studied by psychiatrists that father is often totally absent from such delinquent families; and if he is there, he is frequently an unsympathetic and sometimes a terrible figure.

One of the earliest and most thorough investigations of the family background of delinquency was that undertaken by Robert Andry.[6] Taking a group of eighty delinquent boys and eighty non-delinquents who all belonged to working-class families in south London, Andry examined the father-mother-child relationships in the background of all of them. What he did not find was any evidence that the delinquents had experienced separation from mother, or separation from father. But what he did uncover was that the relationship of the delinquent boys and their fathers was a largely unhappy one. When asked which parent loved them more, the non-delinquent boys said that they were loved equally by both parents; the delinquents unhesitatingly stated that their mothers loved them more. There was no statistical difference in the amount of time the mothers of both groups of boys spent with them—Andry found nothing to suggest that the working mother presented any hazard to her son. But there was a marked difference between the amount of leisure time the fathers of the delinquent boys managed to make available to do things with their sons and the time that fathers and sons spent together in the non-delinquent group. The fathers of the delinquents also seemed to have small idea of what to do with the little time that they did spend with their boys—they did not share hobbies, make things, or visit things together. The delinquent boys saw their fathers not only as lacking in affection, but as lacking in cheerfulness, lacking in praise and too strict and bullying. The fathers' strictness, far from bringing their sons to heel, simply increased the atmosphere of tension and incipient rebellion. Andry was clear in concluding: 'It was the inadequacies in their fathers' roles, rather more than in their mothers' roles, that served to differentiate delinquents from non-delinquents.' His attempted explanation was that 'a child who perceives his father in a negative way over a period of years may gradually not only develop hostility towards the father but may also at a given time start to project such hostility beyond the family scene onto the world at large.'

The Andry survey was published over fifteen years ago. But despite the interest it aroused in professional circles, there has been very little sign that popular opinion has shifted to take in the basic logic of the family situation. If father is to be claimed to be a significant figure, as important in his way to the development of the children as mother, then his position carries with it the same responsibilities. The same pressures need to be applied to small boys that have traditionally been applied only to girls; to train them from the earliest age for good parenting. When a father knows how to be a loving figure, his influence can be immensely to the good; but from the studies of Andry and many others it looks as if a bad father gives a child the worst of all worlds. The children themselves seem to recognise this. Boys on the fringes of delinquency will often give grudging praise to their mothers and the efforts they have made for them, but what they have to say about their fathers can be unprintable. 'There is evidence', says Margaret Wynn in *Fatherless Families*, 'that a very inadequate father is worse than no father at all.'

A poetic attempt to describe the confused and destructive mind of the delinquent and to link it with what he may have lacked in fatherly guidance has been written by American psychiatrist Wolfgang Lederer. In *Dragons, Delinquents and Destiny*, he casts father as the 'dragon' of the title, the strong figure whom the young child or indeed anyone else can perceive to be capable of violence and destruction but who gives an example of how to contain his energy and turn it to constructive ends. In the most obvious way, a father conveys this to his son by restraining him and teaching him self-discipline. 'Father, being strong, can control the child's destructiveness. Father, controlling himself, shows the child that it can hope to control itself.' But much more significantly than that, father gives his son a strong identity. Not that being called Jacobson, McNamara or Ben Akiba defines your clan and role in life in the sense that it once did. But a capable father defines the values and goals of his son firmly enough to make him very sure of who he is and where he is going. His son may merely wish to copy and live up to such a father, he may wish to rebel and supplant such a father, he may wish to be everything in life that his father was not. But one way or another, his father gives his life a context, a sense of destiny, and a meaning. 'He may wish to become a dragon slayer', says Lederer, 'or to become the dragon itself.' But what of a society without dragons? Where father may have been ineffectual, or simply leaves the family? What happens if a father who has been invested by his son with all these mythic and heroic possibilities suddenly disappears? 'Father can fail', Lederer goes on, 'by failing to be strong; by being sick or corrupt, or good and ineffectual, or by dying. If he was the source of a sense of security, then his sickness or death, produces an inner and lasting sense of insecurity. If he was the arbiter of right and wrong, then his corruption produces confusion and despair.' From father's collapse, his son receives the impression that becoming an adult is neither desirable nor safe: he therefore has no future. It is such adolescents, argues Lederer, who become candidates for delinquency.

> The boy has no idea how to be effective himself, having no effective model. He expects the whole world to give to him in a maternal approach. They all start out that way, but they must grow up from mother's to father's domain. And there they must accomplish. The delinquent is not inspired at the thought of joining the grown up world, but intimidated. There are no meaningful goals, and without such attainable goals to mark out the future, the empty time-space is terrifying. There is no point in long-term effort, no point in waiting; the only two tenses are now or never.

Finally the adolescent boy's feelings of impotence and confusion lead him to violence. Many of these violent feelings, Lederer suggests, may be directed towards women. 'The decline of father and the survival of mother may raise the suspicion that mother caused father's death, that she is a spider woman, with whom one is safe as a child but not as a man.'

This paternalist poetry, however, does not have to be swallowed whole. There are insights which Lederer offers. But, in dealing with delinquency, everyone is liable to clutch too readily at any straw in sight. The association between boys with father problems, background poverty and delinquency once seemed so clear that 'social prediction tables' were drawn up to indicate which boys in any area were in danger of turning into delinquents, so that social workers could concentrate their energies on them. One of the cities where this table was used was New York. However, the New York Youth Board was on one occasion surprised and delighted to find that twenty Negro boys in their city, who had everything to complain of in terms of poverty and problems with father and who had been predicted to become delinquent, did not in fact do so. 'Why on earth not?', the New York Youth Board very intelligently asked, and studied the home background of each boy to find out. The answer came from the very high quality of maternal care that all these boys were getting. 'In these cases,' reports a Children's Bureau survey,[7] 'it was evident that the mother, or occasionally the grandmother, had been very active in maintaining supervision.'

But even if an adolescent boy does not get pushed into violence and criminal behaviour, he may still suffer from a milder, but only marginally less miserable, inability to find his place in the world. There are many kinds of social confusion that do not show up in the crime statistics.

The kind of boy who finds life easy, who gets on well with other boys at school and at play, is probably one who is exuberant and mildly aggressive, good at games and other tests of toughness, and generally considered a 'real boy'. In fact at certain periods of their development, when the word 'girl' is used only as an insult, being sufficiently boyish is a basic qualification for just being tolerated by companions, let alone being popular. Boys who seem to be naturally at ease, able to take the lead, popular with their fellows and liked by teachers, do seem to come from very different family atmospheres from other boys who always find life heavy going. The confident, popular, easy-going leaders have been identified as boys who have good relationships with their fathers, who admire their fathers and see themselves growing up like them. A good father-son relationship, it might be said, is the recipe for a straightforward life, if not necessarily a very interesting one.

And it certainly seems to help a young man come to grips with girls. That the over-mothered boy can have homosexual problems is well known. Feelings towards women can turn to awe or hatred, but seldom to lust if mother is too strong. But the fatherless boy who feels healthily desirous of women may not know how to cope with the other sex. Because he has not watched his father teasing his mother, loving his mother, hating his mother, quarrelling and making up, he is emotionally unawakened. Nothing in his experience has prepared him for the marital tug of war. Bewildered and exhausted, he may simply try to withdraw from his wife's attempts to get some reaction from him. 'Our marriage is always so frantic', complains a young husband who had spent almost all his childhood with a widowed mother. 'My wife always seems to be clutching at me, expecting something from me that I can't understand. I try to do the right things, like buy her flowers, buy her jewellery, but that doesn't seem to be what she wants.' Among college students in the United States, boys without fathers certainly seem to have more than their share of troubles with girls. Young husbands whose fathers had died before they were twelve years old were reported by one study to have the greatest problems in marriage, and were described as immature and lacking in human warmth; their sex life was not very active. Much more positive marriage prospects were reported for husbands who had lost their fathers after puberty.

How far the loss of a father or the lack of any attention from a father can contribute to emotional and mental illness later in life is another vast area of research that has only begun to be worked on. Bad fathering can certainly and provably cause mental illness, just as bad mothering can. But what of the effects of no father? There are some indications that sexual anxiety has been found to be more severe in adolescence. Loss of a parent before the age of four or later in adolescence has been linked with depression in adult life, and neurotic and psychotic disorders are statistically more common with individuals who have suffered the loss of father through separation and divorce than for other groups. But in trying to trace links between father-absence and mental illness, the charges are so serious and the evidence as yet so scanty that it is best to consider nothing proven. In family emotional illness, father's place has not yet been examined carefully enough to know what he may be contributing to any sickness by his presence or his absence. Nor has much work gone into what he might be able to contribute to restoring the family back to health. John Howells, director of the Institute of Family Psychiatry at Ipswich, has complained of how little fathers are involved in a positive way by medical and social workers:

> Saddest of all, father's place as a compensating factor, as a benevolent influence, as a therapeutic agent is ignored. Elaborate measures outside the family may be made to compensate a child for deprivation or mothering, when a simple re-allocation of roles within the family may produce

an equally satisfactory, or a better result. It was no ill chance that a child was given two parents; one was meant to compensate for the other.

But even the simplest view of psychological cause and effect acknowledges that anxiety can be the result of a worrying life. The fatherless child can develop a crisis mentality, by having to face too many crises. The one-parent family that is always looking for somewhere to live, trying to balance a precarious budget, aware that neither mother nor the children can have the clothes and treats that others have, is trapped into the habits of anxiety and feelings of inferiority. In the final analysis, it is not possible to make a total separation between material and emotional security. It is not in fact possible to dismiss father, the provider, as glibly as we first did in the opening paragraphs of this chapter.

By insisting that providing was a role that others might undertake, and inviting father to justify his place in the family in his skill in personal relationships, we were inviting him to a contest on grounds that any woman would always pick. This is where women are traditionally strong. 'How good are you in the child development department?' is a legitimate question to ask father. But it is not the question that he has been trained to answer. His skills, his necessary contribution in influencing his children are there almost despite traditional role indoctrination, not because of them. Father has been brought up to feel his duty towards the family is in the field that sociologists call 'mastery of the environment'. In primitive and industrial, in western and eastern, societies, investigations into father's role have concluded that in the vast majority, father is there to help the family solve its external problems, whether these are building a grass hut or arranging a mortgage. Children who have two parents do not simply have a double insurance against abandonment and accident; they also have harnessed to their interests the skills that, whether they are inborn or the result of indoctrination, belong to the two sexes. If father is not there, the income, the discipline, the grass hut and the mortgage all have to be managed by one parent who, no matter how able, is new to some of the jobs. Very naturally, there are occasional panics. Is it any wonder then that the children may grow up a little less serene?

Father's skill and earning capacity is not merely a material fact, either. Money means power, position still means prestige; a father who is successful and obviously able to conquer in the fight as it is currently fought, confers more than material benefits on his children. If his success is in a field that his son can admire and understand, he can convey that effort is worth while and will be recognised and rewarded, that ideas and ideals are worth pursuing, that achievement means something. Though the sons of some outstanding fathers, as we all know, have been stunted by growing up in the shade of the great oak, there are many, many more sons of ingenious and skilful men who have been inspired by their father's efforts.

Though some young men may be scared at the thought of trying to live up to father, others find it a challenge. The whole idea of 'doing well' in the world is an ideal in which the material prizes are symbolic of something more. Our lives have until recently been over-dominated by the Puritan work ethic, so that many have now reacted against it and become sick of success, of the rat-race and the banal struggle to get ahead. Yet the basic ideal of work well done, of effort rewarded, lives on. Even in the most tolerant commune there is a difference in prestige between the man who produces a well-baked loaf, and the one whose efforts are inedible.

And there is no doubt that the father who 'does well' in the outside world earns a more influential place in the family. One of the most striking differences between working-class and middle-class family politics is the relative position of father. In the middle-class family, father is more likely to be permissive and subtle in his treatment of members of the family, but he is more crucially involved when it comes to making an important decision. In working-class families, it is much more often the case that father makes all the authoritarian noises, but mother makes the decisions.

However, father may need to be moderate even in success. The father who is outstandingly successful and away on business too much of the time begins to lose all his family advantages and become a mere provider again. Father has to be there enough for the family to understand why 'men must work', to feel involved in his success, to see it as an asset in their lives, not a wedge that divides up the family.

The over-working father, rather than the working mother, is

one of our current social problems. In the past century, leisure was a sign of status, and even presidents and prime ministers, corporation chairmen and entrepreneurs found time to lunch at home with their families (as they still do in many other parts of the world). But in the west today a husband and father achieves the greatest prestige by working himself into the ground. The part of society that is not moving towards what Peter Willmott and Michael Young call *The Symmetrical Society*, where family roles are shared and the couple divide their time between producing two incomes and being parents, is at the top. There father is an absent figure, too rushed for the basic business of loving and living. This is a situation that career-ridden American families have had to put up with for a long time; and within the last generation it has been imported into Europe.

Today, it is not only the wives of MPs, traditionally left behind in the constituency while the husband makes his dazzling way upwards at Westminster, who report that the children think 'daddy' is merely a voice who emanates from a telephone. Many politicians of course sacrifice all family life to their demanding work. On occasion, one such as Christopher Chataway may choose to do the reverse and give up his political ambitions to preserve his family's health and sanity. It seems the grossest mismanagement that such a choice should have to be made. But in many other fields now, in international businesses such as the oil world, in journalism, in the giant national commercial corporations, in what were once quiet backwaters such as publishing, the ambitious man finds that one of the qualifications for advancement is almost total detachment from his family. That most recent import from the American business schedule, the working breakfast, is affected by those who wish to prove their dedication.

The evils such an obsessive work schedule can entrain are many. Sons grow up with no great involvement with the man who is supposed to help them land on their feet as adult males; they are presented with a model who passes on the pattern that the badge of achievement in this world is not to have any time to spend with your family. From their fathers, such sons learn not to take fathering very seriously. As for the fathers themselves, though elusive to their families, they are powerful presences in society. What they decide on the issues of the day can affect the lives of thousands of people. Some of the decisions they make seem only too evidently to have been arrived at by men who have forgotten what ordinary human life is like.

five The Case for Father: Fathers and Daughters

The decline of father may well be the best thing that has ever happened to girls. The current generation of feminist writers have found their voice partly because fathers have not been around in sufficient force to tell them that it might be unladylike to shout like that.

There is no doubt that a loving father can be as powerful and ambiguous an influence on his daughter as a loving mother may be to her son. But even with the best will in the world, fathers seem to find it difficult to have ambitions for their daughters, to envisage them setting out to conquer new fields. A few fathers in history have egged on their girls to be brilliant—like Sir Thomas More and his Latin scholar daughter, but they are the more famous for being rare. There are contemporary fathers, now, who focus their ambitions on their daughters. Mrs Margaret Thatcher, the leader of the Conservative Party, pays homage to the encouragement of a humbly born, driving father. When a magazine wrote of her as a possible first woman prime minister for Britain, a corrective letter later had to be printed: 'for six years the press has referred to Shirley Williams, Minister for Consumer Prices, as likely to be the first British woman Prime Minister. Mrs Thatcher is not Prime Minister yet and the other choice should not be forgotten.' The letter came from none other than Shirley Williams's father.

But such fathers are the exception. By and large the centuries of patriarchy, of a world run by fathers, have been centuries that have put women down. Today the feminist press is busy publishing details of these long years of paternal blight. While inspiring their sons to aim for the stars, fathers have reared their daughters just to fit in. Most fathers, says one family psychiatrist, want their daughters to grow up 'docile and

72

marriageable'. And generally their wish comes true. Girls who have affectionate contented relationships with their fathers, surveys show, are less likely to have aspirations for a career outside the home. No wonder that most feminist leaders have only one attitude to patriarchy: that it should be overturned.

But if father can often be accused of deadening his daughter's aspirations, flattening her creativity, and making her timid about actually doing anything, does he have any benign influence at all on the girls in the family? Does it matter at all for a young girl if her mother's marriage breaks up and they both return to live with grandmother? She may well get an overdose of protective mothering as a result; but is there anything she will lack? Although this is a situation that arises often enough today, the father-daughter relationship is another aspect of father's role that is almost totally ignored by psychologists. But from what little research has been done, it is easy to see that a daughter's needs in the family are very different from her brother's. A strong father who can keep a son in necessary check, can easily squash a daughter and make her timid and lifeless. The more powerful and effective father appears to his son, the more he adds to his confidence and desire to grow up like father. In much the same fashion, a girl profits from a competent mother. Households where mother dominates may have dire effects on the sons, but observation suggests that they act like rocket fuel on daughters and blast them clear of the conventional underexpectations about life that so often inhibit girls. Girls learn by seeing what mother does and what she relishes. Recently, Antonia Fraser (the biographer of Mary, Queen of Scots), explained the fascination it exerted on her when, as a girl, she used to go into the study of her mother, Elizabeth Longford (biographer of the Duke of Wellington) and find her 'writing and so obviously enjoying it'.

If mother appears to make at least 50 per cent of the decisions around the house, if mother's voice is powerful in working out the family budget as well as the week's menus, if mother has a busy and perhaps even distinguished career of her own, chances are her daughter will not grow up anticipating her own future as one circumscribed by children, church and kitchen. In two-career families the children do not have rigid ideas about who does what, because they see anyone doing anything.

This very situation—a two-career family—is one in which mother is the innovator, inventing ways, sometimes on a desperately day-to-day basis, of how the whole load can be managed. Father often continues with his own work very much as he has always done, though responding to mother's load and chipping in to help. But as Robert and Rhona Rapoport say in their survey, *Dual-Career Families,* 'it is the wife who is the pioneer'. Like all pioneers, she can generate a fervour that the children notice.

By the very nature of what mother is doing, by her flexibility and assertion that who does what in life need depend only on who is good at doing what and who likes to do what, she is poaching on father's traditional territory. Father has always stood up for the division of labour by sex; father always insisted that there are roles and expectations for boys and girls to adapt to differently. Mothers are more even-handed; they are just as likely to get sons and daughters to help in turn with making the beds and carrying out the rubbish. The unisex character of much of our present life is a tribute to mother's overriding influence. And in many of today's busy, two-career families, mother's view tends to make more practical sense. As a public relations director and mother of three explains, when she gets home from the office, sometimes before and sometimes after her husband, it is just as likely to be her sixteen-year-old son, Paul, who is making the spaghetti sauce ready for supper. All the family know the recipe, and it can be anybody's turn to cook it.

This is not the way father has always seen it. His position, and the structure of the traditional family, has always depended on separating out the sexual roles, and pretending that men and women are more different than they are. Father has always been interested, as Talcott Parsons has illustrated, in making sex distinctions. He prefers to ask his son to do the 'outdoor' jobs like taking out the rubbish, a heavy and dirty job, and his daughters to make the beds or cook, indoor tasks which involve caring for people, and which are, father has always said, more suited to her constitution. Possibly fathers are here being unconsciously protective of their sons' future. Some primitive heritage lingers that instils in men the feeling that a woman's future role is so straightforward and obvious, her power so secure; his daughter, he thinks, will feel no anxiety about stepping into the mother role herself one day. Whereas the future role of his son, as an achiever but also as a father, is all in doubt; it is so much harder for the boy to grasp. So father, perhaps, tries to make the whole business more comprehensible by maintaining stricter sex role stereotyping.

Fathers not only separate out what their male and female children do, but they themselves behave differently as parents depending on whether they are reacting to a son or a daughter. They have physical reasons for not treating their sons and daughters the same. Most are chivalrously aware that a daughter could not take the same beating as a son. So they may wallop their sons, in extreme cases, but tell their daughters off. But fathers also expect their daughters to be sociable and articulate, even from an early age, while they encourage their sons to be physically aggressive and independent. In studies of nursery school children, sociologist Evelyn Goodenough[1] concluded, 'the father has a greater interest in sex differences than the mother and hence exerts stronger influence in general sex-typing.' So fathers admire, and therefore encourage, the way the boys climb trees and the way the girls dress up; they give the boys roller-skates for Christmas and the girls a dolls' house. The boys do better out of the deal. Without necessarily understanding it as such, father is passing on a system of male dominance and female subservience. His sons grow up realising that a lot is expected of them by the word 'masculine'; and his daughters grow up knowing how little is expected of them by the current definition of 'feminine'. In families where father's influence is not strong, where father is not around or where mother has seized attention through her own exertion and success, the boys may grow up less aware of the pressures on them to put in a 'manly' performance; but the girls are launched without having already learned the bitter lesson that there are so many things in life that girls do not do.

As a teacher of the traditional sexual roles, which he could be forgiven for seeing as the cornerstone of civilisation, father can be a doubtful blessing to his daughters; but as an individual to love and understand, he suffers from no such handicap. Father is, after all, the first man a girl ever loves. He is the man who first makes her feel her mother to be a rival, and enact the famous triangle of love and jealousy that Freud has pinpointed as crucial in emotional development. And father, above all, is the first man who shows her men. If boys suffer in their early years from too much of mother's and a woman teacher's attention and find it difficult to realise that this is not the sex that they must join, girls in some ways have an even more subtle problem. Because they are reared and taught in their early years by women, and realise very early that they will grow up to be just like mother one day, there is very little motive for them to find out at all that another sex exists. They can live quite cheerfully without knowing that there are men. It is father who has to represent for them this extraordinary and different kind of human being.

Specialists have observed the difference between boys and girls playing with dolls. The small boy, especially if he has a father, introduces a father-doll into the game. The little girl is quite content to play simply mothers and babies. It is as if she returns to a state of primitive matriarchy, and father has to prove to her all over again that there are fathers. Taking in the existence of two sexes, and understanding that they have two different points of view 'is especially important for the female child', writes psychologist Philip E. Slater, 'since the father is more remote and difficult to identify with.' It is much easier for a malicious or simply unhappy mother to obstruct her daughter's feelings for her father; if she conveys to the young girl that men are frightening or despicable or simply inferior, and the father does nothing to break through to his daughter's understanding and win her sympathy, a girl may grow up permanently unable to understand or to tolerate the masculine point of view.

An open-minded and loving relationship with her father, on the other hand, can lay the foundations for many of a girl's later sexual attitudes, and consequently for her success with men for the rest of her life. Girls who get on well with their fathers find marriage easier. This is the benign way in which fathers can 'encourage their daughters to be feminine'. The young girl learns that she is female by learning that her father is male. She does not join him, as a son might do, but sets out to seduce him. The frankly flirtatious manner of a three-year-old girl towards her father is something that strikes even the least observant. She learns how to live with father in all his moods. If she misses out on this experience, she may never quite understand what men are for.

Many of our contemporary heroines, such as Marilyn Monroe, symbolise this predicament; they convey a sense of emotional confusion the more easily from their own background of fatherlessness. A certain exhibitionism, a certain man-hungry quality that father-deprivation can produce, particularly if housed in a pretty physique, often proves fascinating to men—at least for a time. But as men get more experienced, they get more knowing. Film critic George Melly once wrote, when describing Liza Minelli as the father-deprived Sally Bowles in *Cabaret*, 'At seventeen I dreamed of meeting an easy, vulnerable, complicated, perverse girl like Sally. By 46 I've met several, and know to start running.'

If the first experience of loving across the sexes is missing, a girl can grow into a young woman who needs adulation from men but can never really know how to love them. She may live in a cocoon of Prince-Charming-type fantasies about the opposite sex, seeing men as creatures of glamour and power, but finding it very, very hard indeed to appreciate that they are people. The wrath that is at present directed against men who merely use women as sex objects might as justly be turned against women who frequently do not even wish to use men for sex; they simply treat men as things.

And the psychologists would say that what was missing in these women was any experience of affection towards and from their fathers. A small girl and the woman she later becomes lack some basic sexual understanding if she has not had a loving father to play with and cope with, to get angry with, to be admired by and to admire in turn.

In fact some recent theories have gone a great deal further than this. Sexologists have claimed that a woman's relationship with her father is highly influential on her later capacity for sexual play and full orgasm. Alex Comfort once noted:[2]

> The greater a woman's conviction that love objects are not dependable, and must be held onto, the poorer her capacity for full response. This may come about through loss of a father, or childhood deprivation of the father's role. Some degree of parental seduction at the unconscious level seems to be necessary for human females to establish full function. Deprived of a stable father-figure, the non-orgasmic seem to

be unable to face the blurring of personal boundaries which goes with full physiological orgasm. It looks as though sexual response in women is based on pre-sexual learning, and of a specific kind . . . This very important finding about the attitudinal basis of sexual contentment ought to be a salutary check on the idea of fatherless upbringing as a contribution to Women's Lib, an idea which no primatologist would regard with favour. Fathers are there to imprint girls for sexual adequacy.

If father is away, if mother is living on her own or back with grandmother, this just does not happen. The little girl who is deprived of her father in her early years will try to get as much attention as she can from grandfather, uncles and cousins. As a teenager, there is a chance that she will join the 'boy crazy'. Such excessive sexual interest, writes Henry B. Biller,[3] 'may be a manifestation of frustration associated with the girl's unsuccessful attempts to find a meaningful relationship with an adult male.' Later on, she may become highly skilled at provoking the masculine attention she craves, but not know what to do with it once she has got it.

Women who have no experience of an unshakeable and reliable affection from their fathers often find it hard to believe that a husband or a lover is serious. 'You don't really love me', is the plaintive cry of thousands of women who are so convinced that men cannot love them, or do not love at all, that they go out of their way to provoke their partners into dislike or apathy. Such women use many and various ways to test and try their husband's or lover's reactions; a bout of sexual promiscuity, spendthrift extravagance or domestic incompetence may end with the women feeling, 'he can't ever love me after that.' If this does finally prove to be the case and her husband or lover departs, she feels the slight triumph of having been proved right. 'I knew it all along', is the only satisfaction she is able to get.

A lot of women who have never been given a glimpse of how the sexes might blend together simply live miserable lives. But others are pushed over into the only area of criminal behaviour that has traditionally recruited women, that of sexual destructiveness. The girls who never get beyond the simple equation that they have got something that men want—sex, and that men have got something that they want—money, are all set to marry for money, to take to prostitution or, as one survey suggested, to join the thousands of bored strippers who flit from club to club. After interviewing a sample of 35 out of the estimated 7,000 strippers in the United States, two American sociologists reported that 60 per cent of the women came from homes where father was unknown or absent most of the time, and that in baring their bodies to strangers, the strippers were possibly asking for the male attention that they had never found before. When they wanted affection, the women turned to each other—the rate of lesbianism among strippers was estimated by the women themselves at between 50 to 75 per cent.

Women are now taking to crime in increasing numbers, and, freed from traditional role limitations, finding the possibility of being destructive and criminal on a more ambitious scale than ever before (the liberated woman criminal is more likely to see herself as a bank robber or a terrorist than as a prostitute). Moreover the female criminal, like the relatively rare lesbian, is associated with missing father or responding to perverse fathering. One British study among the population of a women's prison reported that over one third of the women prisoners were fatherless for one reason or another. Psychologist Felix Brown commented, 'it is hardly an exaggeration to say that women's prisons are institutions for the aftercare of fatherless girls.' But a bad father, a violent or puritanical father, an exploitive, derisory or hopelessly incompetent father, has the most devastating affect of all. The overbearing or domineering father often incites rebellion in his son, but he is likely to crush his daughter into a fearful submissiveness. The kind of father who despises feminine qualities, goads his wife and pours contempt on his daughters can make it impossible for the girl to grow into any acceptance of her feminine mind or body. Henry B. Biller sums up the results of current research which has 'found that girls who feel devalued and rejected by their fathers are more likely to become homosexual than are girls whose fathers are warm and accepting.' The father who wants his daughter to be the son he never had is the most extreme form of such perversity. Radclyffe Hall, who wrote the notorious lesbian novel *The Well of Loneliness* early in this century, described an upper-class childhood in which she was made to dress, ride and hunt as a son alongside a father who could not accept that she was female. That such paternal influence provokes lesbianism is not surprising; it produces girls who never want to see another man in their life.

For girls, as for boys, to live with a terrible father is the most damaging of all possible family situations. But there is some evidence that living with parents who are not sadistic or rejecting but very unhappily married can produce a greater blight over the growing girl than over the boy. Perhaps because girls are thought to be specially sensitive to personal relations, the conflicts between father and mother seem more often to leave dents in their personalities. The kind of husband who contradicts everything his wife says, changes her decisions and takes every opportunity to degrade and humiliate her in front of the children is bringing up his daughter for the psychiatric ward. In such a situation divorce may seem a positive benefit, and many women and their children have found it so.

But for a mother to retire wounded from the sexual battlefield and nurse her daughters to her is a solution that leaves her with a new set of problems, including an inheritance of doubt, dismay, and perhaps contempt for men, and the conviction that women have to shoulder the burden alone. How can she convey anything hopeful to her daughters about what men are like and marriage can be? If she passes on her own undiluted unhappiness she can put her girl off men for ever. If she tries to cover up and assure her daughter that she will have better luck, she is instructing her to 'do as I say not as I do'; children are never able to pay any attention to such advice. Their mother's real experience is the lesson that they will take to heart.

Such daughters do not grow up 'butch' and masculine. Quite the contrary. They frequently have an inheritance of ultra-femininity. As in the novel *Little Women*, theirs is a world that does not include, or makes only shadowy reference to, men. The real warmth and colour and vitality is confined to the warm maternal burrow. Such a background has produced some big women in its time as well. The passion of Colette, the French novelist, for her mother, 'Sido', may well have been the inspiration of the world of Claudine, of Gigi, of Julie de Carneilhan. In Colette's novels knowledgeable women, appealing young men, clothes, flowers, food and wine are described by the most indulgent female eye ever to direct a pen. Throughout her works, Colette's women are creatures of immense complexity, intelligence and power; the male characters are pets. Charming, alarming and sometimes vicious in their habits, but pets; and in many cases, quite literally kept by the women.

Colette expressed with genius what many others are able to express with blind resentment; that female reactions and interests and delights are the ones that have to be taken seriously. This is the 'derogatory attitude towards males' that psychologists detect among daughters in fatherless families. In Biller's words, 'a very high level of femininity may be associated with a rigid sex-role development which devalues masculine activities.' Among such girls, there has been no chance for any 'identification with father' to take place, no chance for the girl to understand and sympathise with masculine preoccupations and values, to share some intellectual experiences with her father, and to broaden out other aspects of her own personality.

In some families, life without father has acquired its own stability and its own traditions. In many parts of black society in the United States, and in immigrant families in Britain, a high proportion of families survive without a permanent male figure. Mother, grandmother and aunts all convey to the children, not perhaps by words but by their own behaviour, that men are interesting but not to be relied on for the serious business of life. From what the growing girl sees, she may come to the conclusion that all of the real responsibility is shouldered by women. She will be subtly trained therefore to grow up and take on the whole burden, for her own life and the life of her children. If the father of her children does not marry her, or later deserts her, it will fit into the expected pattern; men are light creatures, the women will carry on alone. The cycle is self-perpetuating. Says one American psychologist, 'maternally based households seem to become like family heirlooms—passed from generation to generation'.

Such girls live a mirror-image of the kind of upbringing that many upper-class European males have always experienced; boys who are sent away at an early age to a one-sex boarding school, continue at a one-sex university, and perhaps go into the army, to continue a life in which feminine values and talents are for ever to be despised and misunderstood, and women to remain creatures of mystery. The failure of such men ever to become rounded human personalities is now recognised. What is much less accepted is that daughters who live alone with their divorced mothers and grandmothers and aunts are risking a similar danger. They have a very strong sense of their own powers as women; but they never learn how the other half lives.

A return to the primitive mother-child society is certainly a recipe for capable women. Mother's ascendance and father's decline leads to a system of child-upbringing that is strongly biased in favour of girls, a bias that gets strengthened with each generation. To view such an upbringing with total calm, however, is to accept a world of increasingly strong women and progressively ineffectual men.

six FATHERS without FAMILIES

Anyone who lives near a zoo or an amusement park, or who works in or runs a family restaurant, is aware every Sunday of the appearance of a figure who is as much a creation of this century as any astronaut; the divorced father. Once every two weeks, and generally on Sundays, to fit in with everyone's work and school schedule, he has his children for the day. There he is, chatting with them like a polite and slightly embarrassed schoolmaster, while they gobble their ice-cream or shriek at the monkeys. If he was the kind of father who found it difficult to relax and enjoy his children while he was married, he is even more baffled now. How do you get close to anyone one day a week? And what on earth do you all do?

Fatherless children have aroused sufficient attention by now for some of the right questions to be asked about them by doctors, family health workers, psychologists and social planners. But when we come to the subject of father surviving without his children, even the questions have not been formulated. Father on his own, as he so frequently is after a divorce; father starting a new marriage but trying to keep in touch with his children who live with his first wife; father separated from the girl he was simply living with and trying to find legal grounds to see his son, to whom he has no written rights: there are many such men in existence today, but their problems are seldom referred to, let alone studied systematically. So far there is no guidebook to tell father how to maintain loving relations with the children who are in their mother's custody; there are few psychologists who have asked what emotional deprivation father may suffer away from his children; there are few lawyers who know very much about helping those who have lived together outside marriage and only recently decided that their children have anything to do with the law.

The vast majority of people presume that a divorced father does not have any family problems or family ties. As one embittered father complains, 'if you told any happily married woman that her husband had no interest in the children she would be shocked. But that is what she herself believes the day after she divorces him.'

The only way to discover the peculiar problems of the divorced and separated father, or of the unmarried father, is to use the simple journalistic method of going out and asking them. Such fathers have for a long time been easy to find, and the task of enquiring into their confusions and problems has recently become even easier. For, like everyone else with a social grievance, they have learned the value of banding together for mutual support and to get their views taken seriously. In the autumn of 1974, a number of divorced and discontented fathers, who had lost custody of their children and were finding the basic practical question of meeting and visiting them increasingly difficult, banded together to form a pressure group under the title 'Families Need Fathers' to get their difficulties aired. They soon discovered that similar organisations existed in the United States, in France, in West Germany and in all the Scandinavian countries. In every case these societies had been formed by men who had been hit by the double blow of losing their marriage and their children and who had refused to accept the views of lawyers, judges and social workers that their role as fathers was minor virtually to the point of insignificance, and that their children could be expected to do very nicely without them. In almost every case, they were fighting the blatantly expressed opinions of their ex-wives that if the children did not continue to see much of their fathers it really would not matter. As one former wife asserted, 'The children are mine, all mine. I carried them in my body for nine months. They don't need him. What did he really contribute?'

Not all divorced parents get into this situation. There are many couples who manage to agree, through all the strains and miseries of separating, that, although they cannot live together, they will not deny their children the right to both of the parents that they have already known and loved. From the beginning, they tell their children together about the decision to separate. And although the shock for the children is still extreme, they try to make it appear manageable to their child by showing that they can manage it themselves. Even so, the child will have enough problems. 'I'll never forget', recalls one mother, 'the stricken look on our son's face when we told him, together, that we were separating. I felt, then, that we who loved him were smashing his world to pieces. And I suppose in a sense we were.' But at least such parents try to minimise the hurt. They use their own judgment in settling their children's future, not the law court's. Such couples manage to uncouple, and still remain 'co-parents'. In thinking through the consequences of their actions, they manage to plan ways for the children to do some genuine living with each parent and not merely 'visiting'; for the children to continue to learn and play with, be cared for and worried over by two people, having two entirely different personalities and points of view, belonging to two different sexes and by now living in two different houses.

The right circumstances help, of course. If mother and father still live relatively near to each other, if they have maybe both married again so that neither one can blame their loneliness on the other, they may be able to co-operate over practical details of child-care that prove a benefit to everyone concerned. As one journalist father reports:

> My former wife and her husband live close enough for her to call me when she urgently needs someone to pick up our son from school, and I can sometimes do that and take him home to my house for supper. We can both do things for him fairly spontaneously. There is only one tricky point. Because I am often very busy, my son and I may end up eating in an expensive restaurant, or my present wife and I may have a very well-known politician to supper. If my five-year-old repeats all this artlessly to his mother, she can get a bit annoyed and think that I am showing off to the boy. Obviously, I am not; who shows off to a five year old? But I am aware that this is sensitive territory.

A number of fathers bear witness that they are still the baby-sitter mother turns to first, and that they are very happy to keep things this way.

But the parents who manage to see the advantages of such

co-operation for their children are not perhaps in the majority. Most divorcing couples have generated enough bitterness and distortion over their separation to find it difficult if not impossible to continue to co-operate even over this one final and vital area—the upbringing of their children.

In practice, where poverty so often dogs the divorced mother and limits her capacity to do all she would like for her children, legal tussles constrain the divorced father and prevent him ever getting beyond the first stages of trying to keep up any relationship of great value with his children. After most divorces, mother gets the children (mothers are given custody in 85 per cent of cases in Britain, in 90 per cent of cases in the United States and 80 per cent in France), and father is granted a 'reasonable access' of perhaps two weekends a month, two weeks at Christmas or Easter and two or three weeks in the summer. Father retains his income and the capacity to go on earning, and pays maintenance or alimony to his wife and children. One parent has the children and one has the money. It is a recipe that frequently brings disaster. 'The law puts women into this terrible bargaining position', complains one divorced father. 'I simply had to buy my wife off. I found that whenever I wanted to see the children it turned out to be "inconvenient". When I insisted on visiting the house once, she called the police and had me thrown out. Now I have given my ex-wife everything that she could think of asking for from a material point of view. And I end up seeing the children whenever I want to. But I had to buy that.'

Many husbands, however, cannot pay that price: and this is not what their former wives want anyway. The blackmail may be emotional. A lot of women look at their ruined lives after divorce and see the children as the only thing they have saved from the wreck. They cast their ex-husbands as villains and creators of the disaster. How can they cheerfully hand over the one precious thing they have left to the devil himself—even if it is only for the weekend? The children gradually come to absorb mother's hostility to father; or they find the two worlds that their separate parents inhabit so impossibly difficult to weld together into a rational whole, that in the end they too begin to say that they do not wish to see their father. Divorced fathers tell stories not only of children who have refused to see them, but of children who have been paraded before their fathers with the instructions from mother: 'Now tell your father that you don't want to see him.' The satisfaction that mother gets out of this calculated insult is obvious; what the children may reap from it in the years to come can only be guessed at. For father it is unbearably painful.

Where a total breakdown in communications arrives between the two parents with mother refusing access to the children or insisting that the children do not want it, there is very little that a father can do. The courts can issue all kinds of 'injunctions', but in practice nothing is achieved. Mothers get away with it. They can plead that the children are 'emotionally disturbed', and by now they often are. Mothers can send the children away to school, or on courses abroad. They can move to another house or even to another country. In such circumstances, a father can find it difficult if not impossible to obtain a twice-yearly medical report on his child, to be sent copies of the children's end of school reports, to get any information that will reassure him even that the children are well. And fathers occasionally have well-founded anxieties about the welfare of their children. In some cases mothers are granted custody of the children despite substantial evidence produced in court of their history of mental or emotional illness, despite their remarriage or living with men of doubtful social and medical records.

Many divorced fathers develop a pathological hatred of judges and lawyers, but on occasions it is easy to see why. Some custody decisions seem to reflect a desire on the part of the judge to make amends to whoever he feels is most the victim in the marital conflict, rather than simply to award children a consistent upbringing.

Ken Townsend's marriage collapsed when his wife suffered a severe depression shortly after the birth of their second child, and made several suicide attempts. His parents-in-law, his friends and a housekeeper he hired all helped him to look after the children and keep his job going while his wife undertook treatment in a psychiatric hospital. After two years, Townsend decided he wanted a divorce, shortly after which he married the housekeeper he had come to rely on. Although she was legally merely the 'step-mother', she had looked after both of Townsend's children for so long that she was the mother-figure that they knew and trusted.

A year later Townsend's first wife left the psychiatric hospital and decided to ask for custody of her children. Although her younger child had hardly ever seen her, and her elder child had not seen her for three years, the judge awarded the children to their mother, and suggested to Townsend that he, at least, had the chance of founding a second family. It was a judgment of Solomon, with much to be argued on both sides. The court granted Townsend and his second wife the usual rights to visit the children and have them to their own home, at Easter and Christmas and one weekend a month. Very soon, however, the mother made difficulties about the children going to stay with their father, and after a year she wrote to say that they did not wish to see him again. The elder child is now 'severely disturbed', the father has been told, although no medical and school reports that he asks for are ever sent to him. Visits have ceased, letters no longer arrive. Ken Townsend feels that his children have been amputated from his life. The law, which had the power to give custody to the mother, has proved powerless in enforcing the 'access' it granted to the father.

Of course, the mother had suffered terribly, and wanted her children; of course the children suffered in losing the step-mother who had become the mothering figure they knew; of course the step-mother who had done everything in her power to keep the world steady for these two children when the mother collapsed suffered at having to hand the children over; *and so did the father*. But, Townsend feels, our current assumptions about human nature ignore *his* deprivation almost entirely. He is given no news of his children at all, and no one, lawyer, teacher or doctor, feels at all obliged to ensure that he gets any word to say that the children are well or ill, happy in school or unable to cope. He is treated as a creature without imagination or curiosity.

That men do not lack imagination hardly needs saying, but let one separated father speak for himself:

It is incredible, but true, that my children are living somewhere within a mile or so of me, and going to school in the same area, and short of standing on the pavement and watching them go in with the other children I have no means of contact with them at all. It is a subtle and devastating game that a mother can play once she has established the

breach and separate households are set up . . . and
from lawyers achieve nothing at all. But in all consci
cannot believe that the affections and ties of fourteen
can be suppressed and that the influence I exerted in
particular respects can be extinguished so abruptly with
as much bruising of the spirit on the children's side as, I am
ready to admit, has been caused on mine.

The devastation is complete. Each day begins darkly and
ends darkly, with the centre of my existence having been
taken away. Why the law should seek to deny that men and
their children do co-exist emotionally—in other words love
each other—and pay no heed to the need that each has for
the other in mechanically apportioning the major, if not
total rights to the mother, I cannot understand. There is a
tradition that a man does not complain, does not protest.
This I can understand up to a point in a man's daily dealings
in the world. But to say that this extends to the matter of his
relationship with his children is to strain the rule too far.

The majority of men find it difficult to talk about the
agonies they suffer when they don't see their children. They
have been brought up in the false belief that it is a sign of
strength to be able to conceal emotions, so they try to put a
brave face on personal disaster. This frequently causes women
to wonder if they do have feelings at all. If a mother loses a
child, she sees no lack of dignity in weeping openly about her
bereavement, and indeed weeping all over the front pages of the
newspapers if she feels it will help her. Most men just can't do
this. Even in relatively happy families, fathers often find times
when they cannot express what they feel to their children.
After the disruptions of divorce, at a time when they are
staggered to find out how very vulnerable they are, how little
power they do actually possess in the family, they often go into
a state of shock. Visiting the children every few days during the
weeks when a marriage is finally coming to an end may be more
than father or the children can cope with. Yet if the father stays
away for a while, no one will interpret his actions as tactful or
caring. Mother, children, social workers and lawyers are only
too likely to presume that he has shrugged his family off. And
sometimes he feels this is the least painful solution. 'In some
cases,' says one marriage guidance counsellor, 'the rift between

the parents is so great that the one who leaves the house, often the father, finds his role intolerable and abandons it entirely.' The conventional prejudice is always that women will want to devote their whole lives to their families, and that men want to take to the hills. But an increasing number of men do not see themselves fitting in with these expectations. And more of them are prepared to say so and to try to continue their job of fathering.

Even when divorced parents try to be civilised and responsible about 'access', father's get-togethers with his children can fall far short of parenting. Though the inadequacies of the situation can often make father and children unable to enjoy themselves, there are times when father can become an irresponsible 'treats' man, and sometimes the children love it. Convention gives father a part in disciplining his children, in setting them limits and making them face up to the realities of life outside the sheltered and indulgent family. But a divorced father, who sees his children only on special occasions, inevitably tries to make these meetings into special indulgences. Presents and outings are planned for the children, sumptuous holidays are arranged, and the younger generation can soon begin to ask daddy rather graspingly, 'where are you taking us this year?' Far from bringing his children into touch with the realities of life outside the family, he provides a fantasy life within the family. A number of divorced fathers are well aware of this: as one father complains, 'I would like to find a way to be a father to my children, and not a Father Christmas.'

But mothers can be bitterly aware how much cosier is father's fantasy relationship with the children than the tedious reality they sometimes have to cope with themselves. As a divorced mother relates in Alison Lurie's latest novel, *The War between the Tates,* her rebellious teenage children

> support, or at least prefer, their father, who now makes almost no demands on them and enforces no rules, whom they see for only a few hours a week over expensive meals. During these excursions, they are on their best behaviour and Brian returns them afterwards with an air of self-satisfaction, praising their improved table manners and their knowledge of current events. At home, however, the

children are as bad as ever or worse; foul-mouthed, untidy, rebellious and disobedient.

Yet some divorced fathers can begin to feel that it is not very possible for them to make any further contribution to child care. Father's minimum role is to supply a second opinion—and in even the most mother-dominated families he is usually asked what he thinks even if mother has already made up her mind what is going to happen. But once he is divorced, any comment from father on how the children are developing is liable to be construed as baleful criticism, not to say sniping. Of course it is easy for father to do just that—to take the children for a weekend visit and return full of complaints—that the children don't speak right, or eat right, or indeed do anything the way that he would like them to. But sometimes fathers need to comment; if he is faced with children who seem physically or mentally neglected, who appear to be facing problems that their mother is not aware of, who seem retarded in their development, or in some way arouse his anxiety, he should say something about it. But if he does, his ex-wife is only too likely to find this insufferable. She feels that this is a continuation of a relationship that she has already shown that she finds intolerable; even though this is the last area of responsibility that the two parents are involved in together, they often find it impossible to share it. In a number of cases, the moment father has commented on the children's progress, he has found that access to them from then on becomes impossible. As one father relates: 'Christmas, two years ago, was the last time I saw my girl. When I remarked to her mother that she should be toilet-trained by five years old—and I checked with local medical clinics to make sure that I was right in thinking this—she became completely unco-operative. I haven't been allowed to see my daughter since.'

The concern that any man may feel for his children will be considered natural and earn approval while he is still married; such feelings do not cease if the marriage breaks up, but from then on the father may be given strong hints that this involvement is inappropriate.

Some men are even able to express a certain cynical amusement at the way society signals approval, then disapproval and then approval again, for their actions, when in fact their behaviour remains remarkably consistent and unchanging. Carl Singleton had been married for twenty years, always thinking of himself as a successful father, if a failure as a husband, when his marriage finally came to an end. His wife had endured several nervous breakdowns, but this time she recovered sufficiently to tell him that she felt their marriage was increasing her problems, not helping her. At about the same time, his business suddenly boomed, and he found himself with enough cash in hand to move out without causing hardship to anyone. He bought himself a house in a nearby town, and was awarded the usual weekend visiting and holiday right to see his teenage children. This, he felt, was the best that could be done to straighten out a long unhappy situation. But when his wife began to complain that the children should not visit him, he overcame what he thought was a totally unfair shift of ground by just going into the house and getting them. After innumerable rows and lawyers' letters, he finally got his wife to agree to what the court had allowed. But, in asserting himself, he felt most people regarded him as more or less a nuisance.

Genial but cautious, Carl Singleton did everything possible to make his children's visits to his house simple family occasions and *cheap*.

> We never did anything exotic, partly because I wanted them
> to feel that this was just an ordinary weekend with their
> father, not some kind of 'treat'. Because I had another
> house, I was able to make it so. But my other motive in just
> amusing the children by playing cards with them, and
> cooking with them, was that I did not want my ex-wife to get
> the impression that I was too affluent. She was always
> looking for an excuse to ask for more money.

Over a period of two years, visits and holidays with his children continued because Carl Singleton insisted that they should. And it was during a two-week holiday at his house that he and the children received terrible news; their mother had been killed in a car crash. The disaster hit them as hard as it would any other family; but because they were all together and still close to each other, they were able to survive it just like any other family. And from that moment, of course, Singleton detected that friends and lawyers changed their attitude to him once again. From being treated as a nuisance, he became once more in everyone's eyes the affectionate, dependable father who, of course, could be relied to see the children through on his own. He and the children, and society at large, had been abruptly reminded of the benefits of having two parents. 'I didn't have to change', says Carl Singleton, 'I just went on loving my children like I had always done. But supposing I had allowed myself to be pushed away, and lost touch with the children. Can you imagine how much harder it would have been for them, and for me, when the accident happened?'

But does mother really have to die for a divorced father to be allowed to be useful to his children, and for him to be regarded by the people he comes in contact with each day as a solid support and not just an irritating drag? Perhaps it is not so surprising that death can seem to some husbands the only way out of the impasse. Although a man does sometimes commit an act of desperate violence against his ex-wife when he has lost custody of their children, mercifully, most men do not turn their aggression so devastatingly against their ex-wives.

When the going gets really rough, however, both sexes fight with their most primitive weapons. Women, when trying to shake off father and any claims he may be putting forward for custody or access, are not above trying to cloud his mind on the subject of his biological contribution. 'Now that she has left me, and she's living with this other fellow, she won't let me see the youngest child because she says it's not mine,' wailed one father at a recent protest meeting. 'What are my rights? What can I prove?' And another at the same meeting related: 'We had a beautiful relationship, and we thought we didn't need to get married. Not even when we had a wonderful bouncing boy. But now she has walked out on me. I have no idea where to find her, and I don't think I am ever going to see my son again. What can I do about it?' Many divorced and separated fathers relate their bitterness towards the new 'daddies' that mother invites in, and their conviction that their money is being used to give mother's friends a good time. Others voice fears for their children's safety. 'I used to take my little son to work with me,' explains one father, 'but then I worked in an office. My ex-wife's new boyfriend works on a building site and he takes my boy there and lets him climb around machines and jump up ladders. He is only four years old and he is going to have an accident if this goes on. But what can I do? My wife was awarded "custody, care and control". I have told the local police. I have told social workers, but they all seem powerless to do anything.

A father's basic feelings of protecting a small child are considered normal and admirable one day, and an interference the next—depending on his relationship with his child's mother. Once separated, his peace of mind depends almost entirely on the sense of responsibility of his ex-wife. In the harsh re-think that follows on a divorce, a number of men begin to feel able for the very first time to express their ideas about what father's role is. 'If a man meets a woman and they marry and have a child, then that family exists and all the divorce laws in the universe cannot de-exist that reality. You never stop being a parent, even if you are divorced,' says one father. 'It is still a family, even though you are living apart. The feeling of responsibility for each other will never, ever go. We all still need to go on looking after each others' interests.'

But fathers as a whole, and divorced fathers in particular, are beginning to wonder if anyone is looking after their interests. As a recent 'Families Need Fathers' manifesto points out:

> From time immemorial, men have left their wives,
> sometimes with good reason, often without. In the absence
> of obvious justification, the law has come to offer some
> protection to the woman. Now the law admits that women
> are just as entitled to leave their husbands but does not offer
> the same protection to deserted husbands. Marriage has
> become a unilateral contract. The law has recognised that
> women have the right to live with any man they choose and
> that children have the right to a mother. It does not
> recognise that children have a right to a father.

SEVEN Living with Mother

So there it is. That is the 'classic' case for father. We have had a look at what father can amount to; at the possible conflicts and problems that may arise for children who have to learn to live without a father or lose contact with a once familiar parent. We have had a glimpse into the miseries of fathers who find themselves cut off from the children who used to run and jump all over their lives.

But immediately the suspicion arises that the 'classic' case for father makes sense only if father makes a classic job of it. If all small boys were reared with a knowledge of the task of parenting, and all grew to be men who undertook it adequately, there would be little to argue about: the case for father would be strong indeed. It is because father is frequently very unlike the competent, warm-hearted man envisioned in the professional surveys that arguments for a paternal presence sometimes tend to fall apart. When social workers meet some problem fathers, their scrupulously balanced words of support can freeze on their lips.

Those who have direct experience of hopelessly inept fathers naturally seek to question much of the evidence so far presented in favour of paternal influence, and to introduce a note of scepticism that is no doubt healthy.

The biological capacity to father children is not after all confined to those men who have achieved some sort of grip on life. So much of the 'classic' outline of father's role seems to envisage a male paragon, an upstanding, tolerant, intelligent, encouraging, firm yet flexible ideal masculine figure in charge of the homestead. To some women this sounds like the most infantile kind of wish-fulfilment. The men they have actually known as fathers have been totally self-centred and unaware of their children; some have been violent, and then sentimental, buying the children presents with stolen money, drinking away the rent, getting the family evicted, and causing emotional chaos. Even shaking him off in a way that will leave her conscience clear may not be very easy for mother. 'Once my doctor told me that I simply must get a divorce,' said one young mother. 'I tried to time it in the best possible way for my husband. I didn't want to hit a man when he was down. The problem was he was nearly always down.' Divorce, the chance to live on their own, has become for these women and their children the shining goal to be achieved one day, the best of all the possible worlds they can visualise. They don't want or need to be told about the implications of 'father-absence'; when father has finally gone, they all breathe a sigh of relief.

Much of the work that has built up the 'classic' case for father, critics point out, has very obviously been undertaken in a framework of ideas that presumed that father was a benevolent essential to family life, and this has coloured the results. How sensible is it to trust surveys of the fatherless which define them from the start as *less*? Is there any point in reporting that children without fathers suffer loss of self-esteem when these children are studied as 'children without . . .'?

Most of the researchers who delve into one-parent families naturally end up finding the problems that they set out to look for. But what if they were open-minded enough to ask, 'do one-parent families have problems?' They might then find that the difficulties of mother-headed families were not more maiming and scarring than those of any others. There is no absolutely ideal family, without some handicap or special stress that is unique to its members. There is no family that is automatically doomed or saved by one gain or one loss. Individuals vary so much that all generalisations about what may happen in family life can be countered with innumerable exceptions. Amid the enormous variety of human experience, we must try to avoid being too banal in our anxieties about the fatherless.

There are dangers in fixing labels on families headed by single parents and making them feel that their problems are uniquely damning. And since so many of the one-parent family's problems are financial anyway, will it ever be possible to sort out which of its disabilities are due to material deprivation and which to emotional deprivation, until the mother-headed family becomes a financially secure concern? Some commentators have suggested that it is the tensions and conflicts before warring parents split up, and the suddenness of the separation and change in their lives, that inflict damage on children, not the later period of comparative calm with mother alone. Living with a mother who is fighting and overcoming the trauma of desertion, living with a mother who is undergoing the strength-sapping drift towards separating can be very debilitating for children. Later on, living with the same mother who has learned to cope spiritedly with her lone situation may not be nearly so bad. But any problems that such children may have later will probably be entered in the 'father absence' column, though the seeds were sown when father was still there.

If the tables were turned, and two-parent families were in the minority, a new phenomenon upon the family scene, social scientists might well be scurrying around to study the special problems of having a permanent male resident in the house, and shock reports would doubtless be pouring from research departments on the very real difficulties; jealousy among infants and excessive emotional demands on mothers; the ill-effects of parental conflict or the spectre of violence in the home.

The gap father leaves if he departs will depend almost entirely on the size of the job he did when he was around. If father only made a minimal contribution, mother may be able to continue quite well on her own. Widows, because they are socially respectable, have long been acknowledged to be capable of making heart-warming and very effective efforts to bring up their children single-handedly. It is only the divorced and separated or never married who have been regarded from the outset as probably not up to it. 'On the whole, in our society the one-parent family has been viewed as a form of un-family or non-family or sick family', write Elizabeth Herzog and Cecilia Sudia.[1]

There are a number of reasons why it would be of advantage to recognise the One-Parent Family as a form that exists and functions, rather than as an aberration. One reason . . . is

that over 5 million children [in the United States] live in
fatherless families. Another is that, as a number of
investigators have discovered, such families can be cohesive,
warm, supportive and favourable to the development of
children.

The dire predictions of paternalist psychologists do not
necessarily have to come true. So much depends on the
individuals concerned, on what they feel to be the emotional
realities, and on the way they view the disadvantages—and
advantages—of their lives.

After a recent newspaper article stressing in dramatic terms
the problems and disabilities faced by mothers on their own
and advising unmarried mothers to opt for adoption of their
children, one woman reader wrote in a letter of passionate
dissent:

Women have been bringing up children without fathers for
centuries, after wars, famines and plagues, and mankind is no
worse off for this. The only wrong thing about it all is the
attitude which induces mothers to feel they are sinful if they
do not part with their babies so that they can be brought up
by a mother *and* father. If I had been given away by my
mother as a baby (and it is being 'given away', whatever the
highflown terms) I would feel far more unworthy,
unwanted, inadequate and deserted, than the benefits of a
mother and father would make up for.

I was deserted by my husband three months before my
son was born. I have two children, a son who is three and a
half and a daughter who is eight. We are a very happy family;
I would say happier than any others we know with or
without fathers. I have more energy because there is far less
work to be done without a man around; we don't have to
rush back from a pleasant outing in time to prepare an
evening meal for a man returning from work. We live life as
we find it; we're free, contented and always busy.

One day these unmarried mothers will have to look back
and remember the children they were advised to give away,
and I believe the pain will be unbearable. Whatever the
struggle, the worry and the lack of money, your own child is
far more important to you personally. The feeling of
belonging even to a mother only, is more important than

anything else. We had our bad times with only a few dollars a week to exist on, but the good times are here now and my children are sharing them with me.

Whatever the conventional wisdom about the benefits of two caring parents for every child, there are women like this reader who have lived to prove that half of this ideal pattern can also survive. Two heads are better than one, says convention; not if those two heads are locked in conflict, reply those with different experience. Father is useful as another adult who can dilute mother's influence, and get between her and the children when she is feeling jittery, or moody or ill, say co-operative parents. But that is presuming that father has emotional tact and sensitivity. Many fathers have none of these qualities. A number of fathers interfere pointlessly when mother is getting through to her children very effectively, and are never to be found in times of real crisis when they could help to balance the situation. Similarly, many people doubt that a mother on her own can give as much supervision, or attention, to her children as two parents dividing the family time between them. But it must be remembered that the nuisance value of some fathers is very high, and that a number of mothers in conventional two-parent families are doing a good job by their children despite father, not with his help.

Even statistics showing that children from broken homes turn up in court and get sent to institutions more often than others need to be used warily. Children in homes torn by parental strife do worst of all.[2] There is also evidence, point out the sceptics, that children from broken homes get treated differently by officials; that the policeman or probation officer is less likely to send a child back to home discipline for a small offence if he discovers there is only one parent. Occasionally, single mothers take their children along to the police and probation services because they fear the children are heading for delinquency, even when their 'crime' is a minor one that two parents together might shrug off. What prevents children from becoming anti-social is the quality of their home life in its entirety; whether father is there is not the only factor. Some fathers drive their sons to delinquency, and in rare cases even offer a criminal training.

But don't children feel humiliated if they don't have a

father? Well, it seems to vary a great deal according to the circumstances. The children of widows seem to survive rather more easily without a father, because he left them in the most respectable and sometimes even honourable of circumstances. If a dead father was a war hero, a test pilot, or an explorer who never returned, children can even feel pride in the honoured gap in the family. And mother's affection towards such a figure, in contrast to what her feelings may be towards a man who simply left her, conveys to the children that their status is something to wear with pride. A dead father also has one other great advantage, some psychologists maintain. He cannot return. There is no chance that he can make a surprise visit and agitate mother and set the children agog. There is no chance that he can get into disputes about 'access' and force the children to share his own distress at how seldom he sees them or how aware he is that the bonds between them all are weakening. A dead father is the essence of tact.

So favourably do the sons and daughters of widows shape up that a group of psychologists have recently suggested that the parent who loses custody after a divorce (most frequently the father, as we know) should do his best to play dead. Normal practice, of awarding custody of the children to one parent while granting access to the other, is based primarily on our ideas of fair play for the adults concerned; what the child needs, argue the eminent British and American authors of *Beyond the Best Interests of the Child*,[3] is certainty. Shipping him back and forward between parents like a parcel is likely to sow the seeds of confusion, to keep the question alive in his mind of why mummy and daddy don't live together, and to increase feelings of divided loyalty and guilt towards both parents. It is asking too much of any child to expect him to love two people who detest each other. If the parents cannot keep up some sort of civilised tolerance towards each other, then it is best that the child should be allowed to love one of them without qualm or disturbance. 'Unlike adults, who are generally capable of maintaining positive emotional ties with a number of different individuals, unrelated or even hostile to each other, children lack the capacity to do so', say these psychologists and lawyers. 'They will freely love more than one adult only if the individuals in question feel positively to one another. Failing this, children become prey to severe and crippling loyalty conflicts.'

In the cause of continuity and certainty, which Anna Freud and her colleagues maintain is of paramount importance for any child, it is argued that the parent who gets custody should of right make all the important decisions about that child's life, including whether or not to allow visiting to the other parent. Father, in other words, may be required to disappear from view.

Such a recommendation takes for granted that mother alone, while maybe less good than mother backed up by father, is certainly more effective than mother debilitated by conflicts with father. And there are many others who question whether the 'classic' view of father's influence really appreciates how frequently fathers prove inadequate to their role. Take the so-called intellectual and achievement bonus of having a father on hand. There is no doubt that, *if father is interested,* he can stimulate his children and plant in them a hunger for knowledge and wisdom. But it is absurd to presume that every father can or is willing to try to do this. Father has traditionally only been interested in the attainments of half his children—the boys—and even then it is often easy to accuse him of training them in some of the more crass aspects of competition, of the commercial or sporting rat-race.

This is not what children need. Nor is it what arouses intense mental or imaginative involvement and effort. What children thrive on—both sexes equally—is a parent who is keen to encourage them in their own highly individual capacities to think and feel, a parent who treats their responses to the world as unique and worthy of attention, irrespective of how they compare to those of other children. It is in this sort of environment that creativity is nourished. And it is at this sort of upbringing that mothers seem supreme; their inspirational gifts are second to none. As their famous children make clear; writers like H. G. Wells and Jean-Paul Sartre, painters like Oscar Kokoschka, sculptors like Henry Moore, and cinema figures like Charles Chaplin all pay homage to their mother's capacity to encourage their individuality and the effect of this maternal treatment on them. Chaplin's autobiography is probably one of the most moving modern documents of childhood; yet, at the end of its terrible story of early years in poverty with an alcoholic father who died of drink at the age of thirty-seven, and a frail nervous mother who entered mental hospitals on several occasions, Chaplin states defiantly, 'in spite of our early poverty, my mother had always made my brother Sydney and myself feel unique and distinguished.'

Yet surely there is one part of the case for father that is above controversy. As a man who can live amicably with mother, he shows his sons and daughters how relations between the sexes can be made to work. And nothing and no one can take his place as a model for his son, as the male figure there before him who teaches him how to be himself and how to be male. But the word 'masculinity' is beginning to be attacked, by men as well as women, almost as much as the word 'femininity' has ever been. When the just revolution against the tedious roles that 'masculinity' and 'femininity' have been allowed to conjure up is finally over, there may still remain however a sense of manliness and womanliness as two distinct and valuable qualities in life. And father can surely be helpful in guiding his son towards manliness, as mother is in presenting a womanly way for her daughter. There does seem to be some testimony that can't be shrugged off, some residue of evidence that without his father, sexual and personal insecurities may remain with the son in adult life. At its most basic, any young male has a right to expect a helping hand into the world from an adult male, and why not from the adult male who engendered him? If it is admitted that much of the behaviour that fathers instil into their sons at the present moment as 'masculine' is not necessarily very desirable behaviour, even if some of it has distinctly fascist overtones, this does not totally discredit father as the teacher of some more intelligent role expectations at a later date. There is no benefit to anyone in deliberately setting the teeth of young males on edge, in denying them fathering and confusing them as to the validity of being men at all.

Some of the confusion that can afflict a fatherless boy may seem to be fairly temporary, however. There are signs that such boys can experience a 'time-lag' in development, a period in which they have to catch up on where they fit in. And though being deprived of a reasonable quantity of masculine influence in childhood may have an effect on a young man's later emotional life, it is by no means certain what that effect may be. The predictions of psychologists often turn out to be wildly inaccurate, as the most intelligent of them are only too willing to admit. Jean MacFarlane looked back over a child development study[4] that predicted adult patterns for a large group of children and then rechecked them as adults; the predictions turned out to be wrong time and time again. One of the errors was in forecasting what would happen to a number of boys who grew up under the influence of dominating mothers:

> One of our predictions was that our over-dependent boys with energetic mothers would pick wives like their mothers and continue their patterns. For one or two we were right, but nearly all of the dependent boys picked for wives girls who were lacking in confidence . . . giving themselves a role as the proud male protector and giver of support. They thrived under this new non self-centred change of status.

It may be that masculine tyranny in adult life is very often a reaction against what was seen as maternal tyranny in the life of a young boy. A generation of dominating mothers may produce a terrible reaction for the women who will come after them. Who knows? People are still much too complex and interesting and contain too much capacity for self-correction to run docilely along the lines that the infant science of psychology may care to predict for them. 'Psychology', as one psychologist recently remarked, 'has merely reached the level of understanding natural to any reasonably intelligent and observant grandmother.'

Obviously living with mother, instead of living with mother and father, will have a profound effect on a child's personality that will continue on into adult life; but exactly what that effect will be can really only be guessed at. Joseph H. Hirschhorn, the American uranium millionaire, has given accounts of his childhood in Brooklyn as a poor Latvian immigrant, dependent on a widowed mother who had thirteen children to bring up on what she could earn sewing at a few pence an hour. Once, when his mother was injured in a fire, there was literally nothing to eat. Such a childhood must have made a young boy desperately aware of his dependence on his mother. Far from turning Hirschhorn into an uncertain social misfit, it gave him the motive to become a highly successful broker at the age of seventeen. Nor was this all. Instead of deadening his imagination, his early years had fired it.

Hirschhorn went on to become one of the most sympathetic and daring of modern collectors of painting and sculpture, always insistent on backing his own judgment and always preferring to help a good painter who needed cash and encouragement rather than to buy an already well-established name. The museum that now bears his name in Washington is the memorial of a man who was spurred on rather than crushed by starting life without father.

What ignites one child, however, may destroy another. The capacity of one individual to triumph over adversity is no argument for recommending adversity for all. But it does bring us back to a very obvious point that can get overlooked in anxious discussions on how children can make out without a father. It mainly depends on the mother. The mother who is there is going to be the crucial influence on the growing children, not the father who is not there. Father's absence, indeed, may be at its most real for the children in the way that he survives in mother's mind, and influences her attitude to the children. She may try to make up for the loss of her husband with over-possessive affection for her children; she may try to avert the development of anti-social behaviour that reminds her of the father by too strict a control of the son or daughter. From an early age the children may have to become 'mother's little companions'. 'I know I forced my eldest boy to grow up too soon,' says one widow, 'but I just needed someone to lean on. He was the closest and most understanding, so it had to be him.'

For as long as mothers are, by and large, the parents who are there most, and whose personalities generally have the most direct day-to-day influence on their children, then keeping mother happy and confident is obviously a basic priority. Many mothers who have been bitterly unhappy and lost all self-esteem while trapped in the conflicts of an unworkable marriage are willing to testify that they can make a better job of child-rearing once they are on their own. Pursuing the line that what's good for mother is good for the children, they argue that because they feel saner without their husbands, the children will be too. 'It's actually easier looking after my son, now that my husband is not here,' says one formerly exhausted mother. 'I used to feel that I was trying to organise two little boys.'

It needs stressing again that if all husbands were good

fathers, it would be easier to take a more consistent view of the problems of life without father. As it is, common sense suggests that father's necessity in the family all depends on the individual who is father. One man may well enhance the lives of his wife and family, and another ruin them. Psychologists' generalisations about father taking the ultimate responsibility and representing the ultimate authority sound like bulletins from an ivory tower when confronted by the variety and chaos of real life. Many men seem unaware that there is a role attached to the name 'father'. And others find they cannot adapt to it. A very young mother with a three-year-old daughter explained, 'we lived a very carefree, hippie existence, until I got pregnant. Then I accepted that my life would have to change, that here would be another human being that I would have to take account of. But my husband couldn't change. He couldn't mature. He just wanted life to go on the way that it was before.' Her marriage ended under the strain. Other women in similar circumstances accept that they will have to do the 'fathering' as well as the mothering. They, at least, have grown up.

After all, how can a father 'make a son aware of the rules of society', if he flouts them himself? How can he be 'the final source of authority' if it is obvious to the children that mother is running them and him? How can he promote a secure and stable life if he is an unstable muddler? 'I feel so much more secure,' admits one divorced mother, 'now that I know that the bills are paid because I paid them, now that I know that promised treats will materialise because I have planned them. I am sure that the children feel more confident about it all too.'

Women are better educated today, and sometimes more knowledgeable and ambitious than their husbands. As one escaping wife related of her sailor husband, 'he hadn't had a good education like me. He didn't think it important, education. I'm glad I left him because his idea for my son was that he should go to sea, and I didn't want him to do that, I wanted him to work with his brain.'[5]

When it is absolutely necessary, when divorce is the only road to real survival, when father is killed in an air crash, when a girl bravely faces the fact that a hasty marriage is not really going to solve the problems set by her pregnancy, then a mother must try to cope alone. She, and everyone else, will already know something of what her burdens will be. Poverty generally—or at least an exclusion from the general affluence; loneliness almost always; exhaustion much of the time. Widows and divorced mothers confess to feelings of incompleteness, to the sadness of permanent loss. They are all aware of the curious single sex world their children perceive. 'I think it is so sad that my children are growing up in a home where they never see a man put his arms round me in affection,' says one divorced mother. Others, who keep loneliness at bay with an attempt at a frantic social life, wonder what their children make of mother's changing cast of 'admirers'. Mothers who never married just stare uncomprehendingly at the majority of women's lives and wonder what it's like. For all of them the day-to-day burdens are appalling, every disaster has to be overcome alone, the leaking roof, the smashed-up car, the childhood illnesses. Sometimes sheer exhaustion and stress bring the mother to her knees and she sinks under the weight of her worries, and then the children are in danger. Frequently she struggles on, neither quite sinking nor swimming. 'Everyone engaged in children's work', writes Margaret Wynn,[6] 'is worried at the way in which so many children come into official care from good mothers in bad circumstances, rather than from bad mothers.'

But when mothers have got some of their practical problems sorted out, when they do manage to keep going, may there even be some advantages? Children who are brought up by mothers on their own are bound to be different, but may some of the differences actually be beneficial?

A house with only one parent in it can obviously have one great advantage—it can be a house without discord. Providing mother is strong enough to know what she is doing there is no one to argue with her. Some lone mothers give the impression of smoothly functioning independent energy. If they have an outing they want to plan with their children, if they decide they want the living-room painted red, they do it. There are none of those 'shall we, shan't we' discussions that end in nothing happening at all, and that reduce many married women to feelings of impotence. There are no family arguments over the children's education; mother chooses what she thinks best. There are no rows over money; either mother can afford to do it or she can't (often she can't, but a relatively simple life does not do children any harm).

Mother's discipline is often of the best kind; she can afford to be flexible and permissive because she is closely involved. She is very aware of how her children are thinking and feeling, so she is not tempted to draw arbitrary limits that do not fit their personalities. Her morality is subtle and personal. Her own example of hard work and self-sacrifice for her children points many of the necessary moral and social lessons. Mother usually talks more candidly to her children than does father about the realities of work and effort, money and reward, the overriding importance of personal life in achieving any kind of happiness in this world, the necessity to keep an open mind and be grateful for what life brings along.

The lessons she passes on express the female mind at work—naturally. And the personalities of her children are very likely to display the influence of traditional female preoccupations. The maternally-reared seem to lend their talents, however limited, to the expression of recognisably female values.

Women pass on to their children their own abiding *concern* about themselves and other human beings. It is no exaggeration to say that much of twentieth-century insight into personal suffering and the wish to see it conquered and personal happiness promoted is part of the assertion of female values. The modern sciences of sociology and psychology, and the vast numbers of students enrolled to study and practise such contemporary attempts at healing, are witness to how well the ideals of maternal care have been imbibed by both sexes. Magazine photographers' work is exhibited under the title 'The Concerned Photographer', and illustrates the attitudes and preoccupations that are currently in fashion. In one century, concern has ousted conquest as the professed ideal of personal and international relations.

The current obsession with 'talking it out', with attempting to solve problems by enlightened discussion rather than by a short sharp fight, is another reflection of mother's method. Discussion and persuasion (which they are good at) have always been viewed by women as morally superior to a clout over the head (which they are bad at). Negotiation, analysis, trying to understand the other fellow's point of view—all now accepted as the civilised way to conduct affairs between individuals or social groups—are techniques that come naturally to the female and the female-reared. 'Confrontation' is frowned upon; appeasement may not be.

Mother's indulgence towards her children's individuality encourages creativity, as we have already suggested and possibly it can inspire previously undreamed-of ambitions as to what people can *be*. Maternal encouragement may well be the source of the whole vision of 'self-actualisation'—the aim 'to become everything that one is capable of becoming', in the words of Abraham Maslow, the distinguished humanistic psychologist.[7] But is it always a vision of self-development or of self-indulgence? Such ambition can perhaps rather easily be twisted to that of spoilt children demanding, 'Life must give me everything that I am capable of wanting.'

And women are notoriously lenient about sexual irregularities. Fascinated rather than appalled by the diversity and variety of creation, they find it difficult to see why homosexuality should inspire laughter or contempt or fear; and in most sexual relations between men and women they judge the morality of events by how much the individuals involved *care* rather than by whether some code of behaviour has been offended. Women, in short, tend to be permissive. The 'live and let live' tolerance of today's world has been directly promoted by the female view.

When mothers are in charge of the family, they are usually very concerned to bring up Tom and Mary to be strong, healthy people but much less concerned to tell Tom to be a man, and Mary to be a woman. Women encourage the merging of sexual roles by refusing to take much interest in separating them out. 'Anybody can do anything' is the slogan that women, usually unconsciously, promote. As our increasingly unisex society now makes plain.

Intellectually, mother's influence tends to be progressive.[8] Theorists who have tried to apply psychoanalytic method to society at large suggest that in societies where women are influential, the word 'new' evokes an instant appreciative response; much as the word 'old' does in patriarchal circles. Tradition—which can be translated as 'what our forefathers did'—is readily abandoned by the maternally inspired avant garde. Women are experimenters, as permissive and welcoming to new theories as to new faces. Mother is the mother of invention, frequently promoting change for change's sake.

Mother's influence is considered to be almost all-pervading today, because of her dominant position in most families. But in the one-parent family obviously she has no serious contenders. The way she instinctively approaches the problems of life and love are accepted by her children as the way things are. It is sensible to prefer the majority of children to be brought up with a knowledge that there are two sides to every question and particularly two different traditions of human values, the masculine and the feminine. But perhaps we need not cry disaster if some children are reared with an inbred appreciation of only one. Many of the qualities that mothers inspire in their children may indeed seem to be peculiarly appropriate to the needs of our present-day world.

Lucky children in this world have a loving parent; and the very lucky ones have two. To have a loving and interested father is an enormous blessing. But no mother who is coping with a family on her own needs to feel that she is merely hatching disaster. Only the convolutions of Jewish humour can perhaps express the exact balance of benefit or deprivation that father can confer or not by his affectionate presence: 'lack of a father is not as bad as having a father is good'.[9]

ЄiqhT FaTHERiNq:
a Daily HabiT

A good father is a blessing; an inadequate father may be worse than no father at all. This is the message that runs all through the investigations that have been done on father's contribution to family life. The suspicion arises that one of the reasons why fathers are now losing out is that they so often prove to be unsatisfactory at the job. Many men are willing to admit that they are not very good at fatherhood, but they are at a loss how to improve. And they can claim with some justification that no one ever gave them the idea that being a father might be an important role, that certain paternal skills might need to be learned. Bad fathering, minimal fathering, may be all that they have ever seen. No matter how dazzling a man's talents in any other field, as a father he may disappoint himself and his wife. Even the most liberated relationships are no defence against this general feeling of dissatisfaction. As Liv Ullmann remarks of Ingmar Bergman's efforts with their daughter Linn, 'He is trying, in his unfulfilled way, to be a father and he's better year by year. He's very nice to her and proud of her. But, of course, he's not like the father I imagined.'

Fatherhood is a job for which there is no training programme. Girls are brought up to look forward to marriage and child-rearing as part of their future achievement. Boys often have it subtly indicated to them that they will be fulfilling expectations if they avoid marriage for as long as possible and take a cautious amount of interest in their children once they arrive. The involved and affectionate father is that rarity, an individual who ignored the general expectations. Or he may be a lucky man who did receive some of the right ideas—from his own excellent father. An easy acceptance of fathering can perhaps be absorbed along with vitamins in

something about oneself is a compliment; it recognises his existence and his curiosity, it encourages it, it helps to satisfy it. It begins to give the adults' comings and goings meaning.

One of the finer tools of fatherhood is a sense of historical perspective. The system in which modern fathers operate, the industrialised society, makes the task of being a father more difficult. In primitive, agricultural communities, adults and their work and their pleasure used to be straightforward and easy for children to learn about. A child was able to sit and watch what father did, and understand readily why he did it; father built the grass hut that the child then sheltered and slept in. Father was seen literally to bring home the bacon. Work and domestic life were closely intertwined, parties and festivals and special celebrations included all age-groups; and all of this life went on in the same, often primitive, buildings. Any child could grasp it. Now that we have stylish houses, towering office blocks, and separate clubs for deliberate pleasure, now that we so often segregate people by age, our split lives not only make it difficult for the adults to pull it all together, it is more difficult for the child to develop a coherent world picture and understand how father's life works. The job of gradually introducing children to a sense of how and why society functions and what men do towards it is no longer one that will take care of itself naturally, it requires thought and planning from fathers.

Father's part in presenting to his children a casual introductory course to the wider world is particularly important because so much of children's education is already in the hands of women. Viewing childhood with some historical perspective reveals that the worlds of home and school have been run too much in the recent past by mothers and women teachers. This is a disadvantage for young boys. During their most impressionable years they come to feel that women are the fountain of knowledge and discipline. In adolescence they can come to rebel against both. In countries as far apart as the United States and Russia, a number of voices have been raised to protest at how few men enter the teaching profession, and to campaign for a more equal balance of the sexes in the classroom. But if father can rise to the task at home, the problem is halved.

Authority—the vexed question of how much weight father's

voice carries and in what areas—seems to be something that is now exercised in highly individual ways in each family. People earn the authority that goes with their talents. Among equals, there are still situations in which one parent becomes repeatedly more equal than the other in the amount of responsibility he or she takes, in the subtle way that the whole family begins to take it for granted that on this issue they can pass the buck to father or to mother. If the responsibility rests with father on financial questions, or with mother on educational questions—or vice versa—then it is only just and natural that the parent who has to solve the problems earns the right to be listened to and, after discussion, obeyed. The special talents one parent develops may be in any field. As one father explains, 'I am a designer and my daughter takes it for granted that she discusses her artwork and her clothes with me.' Children begin to look to each parent for support in very specific areas. Capabilities with children vary between individuals and not between sexes. Father may be the more intellectual parent, and the children may turn to him and listen to him more seriously when they are exploring ideas. Mother may be the one who has a gift for organisation, and can give practical advice over problems the child has set himself. Dividing up the day-to-day tasks can be argued over. But the emotional turmoils and rewards are there to be shared, by men as well as women.

Children are a challenge to any human being's capacity to feel, and the feelings start even before birth. Some of the feelings that are liable to afflict a man when his wife or girlfriend is pregnant can be very disturbing indeed. In the past, it has often been assumed that much of a man's moodiness during this time comes from guilt at having caused his wife's condition, at having put her health in hazard through his sexual appetites. There may still be households where this kind of guilt hangs heavy. But today we are more likely to admit that the edgy expectant father feels a mixture of jealousy and envy.

If this is his wife's first pregnancy, he may have a wise premonition that she is never going to be quite the same again. Parenthood is still what makes the sexes diverge, not necessarily into 'opposites' (as Rebecca West recently said, 'I can easily imagine an opposite sex to women and I can easily imagine an opposite sex to men, but it isn't men and women!'), but certainly into people with some different preoccupations. And pregnancy threatens future responsibilities that are going to compete with their companionship as a couple. 'Do you realise that this is the last evening that we will sit here alone together for twenty years?', one husband asked his wife a few days before the birth of their first child. He may have been exaggerating but no doubt he was merely saying what many have thought. Prospective fathers find it useful to prod similar sore points and face the fact from the beginning that there are two very different life-styles—those that include children and those that do not.

No man should feel any longer that he has to have fatherhood thrust upon him. Men, as well as women, have now been given a genuine choice whether to be parents or not. For some, the very best answer is not to embark on fatherhood at all. As one writer confesses: 'I know that I have been a disappointment as a son, which is the easier role; in the much harder part of the father I have every reason to expect an ever worse performance from myself.' That individuals can now feel free to come to such a decision, and stick to it, is a benefit for everyone.

What is even more revolutionary is that men are now able to discuss their feelings of envy of the maternal role. Primitive tribesmen have always been able to admit that they coveted the limelight and the achievement of giving birth and in many early societies the 'pregnant' husband was treated with great solicitude, put to bed and cosseted through sympathetic birth pains in a ritual known as couvade. Centuries have rolled by when men have had to pretend to be bored or disgusted by childbirth, and only now are we in an era that can be candid about sexuality and allow men to say that they wish they could do it too. 'I think it must be wonderful to carry a child inside the body', one father recently confessed; 'sometimes when my children have been lying on top of me and bouncing around I have had an idea of what it might feel like.'

Conflicting emotions and a sense of impending responsibilities build up into a stressful situation for some men during their wives' pregnancies; a few even require psychiatric care when their worries get totally out of proportion. The majority, mercifully, remain on hand to take an active interest in their wives' progress and to preserve a sensible perspective. In the last months of pregnancy, many women's thoughts very naturally begin to centre on the child inside them. If the husband also shows an interest in the changes that are taking place in his wife's body, feeling and checking with her the movements of the growing arms and legs inside her, it can reassure them both that this is something that is happening to them, that means something to them, as a couple, not simply to her. But he can also help his wife to keep some of her imagination involved with the world outside her body, and by planning for other events ahead, as well as the child's birth, keep in touch with everyday reality.

Not that reality itself does not become strangely heightened at the moment of birth for the mother and father. For the lucky couples who insist that the father be there in the hospital, and for perhaps the even luckier couples who do not have to insist because their child is born in their own home, the actual moment of birth holds extraordinary passion and intensity. Now that giving birth is beginning to be unfashionable, those who enjoy it can say so without being thought banal, as novelist Margaret Drabble has pointed out.[1] Although she cannot find many good words to say for the first stages of labour, 'the last stages', she recalls, 'were spectacular. Ah, what an incomparable thrill. All that heaving, the amazing damp slippery wetness and hotness, the confused sight of dark grey ropes of cord, the blood, the baby's cry. The sheer pleasure of the feeling of a born baby on one's thighs is like nothing on earth.' Even as a spectator, father gets an enormous sensation of primitive satisfaction. And there is plenty of chance for audience participation; fathers are often the first to hold, to photograph, to hand the child to mother. After interviewing a hundred fathers who were present at the birth of their first child, a team of sociologists reported[2] that ninety-three said they would definitely be present at the next birth and made general comments 'about the wonder of nature—sentimentality generally attributed to females', they observed wryly. Unfortunately, in pursuit of hygiene, father has frequently been barred from the birth of his child along with the germs. The moment of birth is too often the first of many bitter occasions when he is left on one side asking himself if they really need him at all. 'I wonder', ponders psychologist Virginia Satir,[3] 'whether it would be possible for men who are fathers to leave their families as readily as they do now if they were part of the literal birth proceedings, openly hailed and honoured as being and having been essential, as are women.'

Certainly, in the first few months of his child's life, it can be a struggle for father to earn any sort of part for himself. For some months, mother and child seem still to be bound by a slowly unwinding umbilical cord. Even the most undomesticated man may find himself decorating a nursery or building a part of a new kitchen during the first few days of his child's life, because he wants to contribute.

Once the child starts on a bottle instead of mother's milk, plenty of fathers find a ready opportunity to get close to their child. Not only do babies find it interesting to look up and see father holding their bottle, but fathers find themselves impressed and learning a lot about healthy physical reactions. The extraordinary pride and pleasure that young infants get out of all their bodily functions, sucking until replete, concentrating on excreting, can be an object-lesson in how to live a healthy life without tensions. For the harassed adult, the infant provides an exhibition in natural living. Whether the adult is able to learn from it or not is a different matter.

Because modern families are small, few adults today have very much experience of children before the birth of their own. We are often astonished to find that infants are people from the word go. The first year of life is the period of greatest growth and development, and can be one of the most absorbing and revealing for any parent. It does not have to be monopolised by the mother, though too often until now it has been presumed that she alone will rock the cradle and rule the nursery world. Now, when fathers become involved with their children from the earliest weeks, they find it more interesting than they ever imagined. No two months are the same. At four months the infant begins to recognise father as not the same as mother, but as a special extra parent. The observant parent notes the precise moment when a small child learns to react to a colour, to pick up a spoon or a ball and hold it firmly; everyone can share in children's infectious enthusiasm at the awakening of the senses by handing them objects to feel, to bang, to drop again and again from a high chair. If a child has learned to trust his developing senses and the two huge people who seem to be encouraging him, his basic attitude to life will have been established as a healthy one. This first year of life also gives fathers a chance for thought and reassessment. To those who are open to the opportunity, being a father can be a spiritual experience too. It offers a man a chance to strengthen and yet relax his own grip on life, to weigh his values and assess what he has really learned about living that is worth passing on to his children. 'Since my son was born two years ago,' says one father, 'I find I am more ambitious and at the same time more satisfied with life, more creative and yet more settled. It has really changed me.' Another new father explains: 'It is some sort of relief that there is another life, which is an extension of myself, and I have really thought about it. I am not bothered if I drop dead tomorrow. That's a funny way of putting it, but I feel as though life is now being carried on.'

And mother has changed too, but not always in ways that are totally to her liking. The majority of women find the experience of placing a new human being firmly on the path to a happy, healthy life to be very satisfying. But in most families, the wife has to pay dearly for this privilege and renounce, at least for a while, many of the other interests and many of the people she knew before their child was born. She may be conscious of the fact that she has less time and emotional energy to spend on her husband also, and he may be very aware of this, sometimes feeling as jealous of his son as he is fond of him. But even the most sympathetic man finds it difficult to imagine totally what this change has been like for his wife. Can he imagine how he might react if he suddenly abandoned his adult routines, his work, his friends and his regular pleasures for a life that for perhaps two or three years was firmly child-centred? He might go crazy, and some women do. The majority, amazingly, are resilient enough to survive, and find a capacity to adapt that they did not know they possessed. In most cases, their husbands are admiring of their wives' many-sided capabilities. But that admiration and even understanding are not enough. One of the challenges of modern fatherhood is coping with modern mothers. At the right moment for her, and for the children, fathers now find they must help to ease mother back into the adult world. At first, his wife may be able to escape from the house and children for maybe only a few hours a week, but he can guide her towards the mother's help, the baby-sitter, the co-operatives of young wives, the play group and the kindergarten that are going to give her some personal freedom. Some husbands are able to take over entirely for a weekend or a week, to give their wives a chance for a visit to a friend or a conference that will keep them involved in the world they knew before motherhood. Fathers who do this sustain some shocks and gain greater understanding while handling the whole burden alone. 'When Anne went away for a week and I had the two children on my own,' says one father, 'I discovered for the first time that it takes about an hour and a half after they have gone to bed to pull my mind together and concentrate on my work, or even on the newspaper. Children seem to expect and even train their parents to have an attention span like theirs of about ten minutes.' Another father agrees: 'I didn't even know I had consecutive trains of thought until I had children to interrupt them.'

A few fathers have come to the conclusion that they can be happy with a fairly straight role-swap, allowing them to take over at home, while mother pursues some strategic phase of her work. Though this is probably not a solution that will ever appeal to the majority, for some couples at some stages it can seem the most natural way round. 'Susan had a job to return to after her maternity leave, and I am still working for my law exams', explains one housebound father. 'It just seemed to make sense for me to work at home and look after the baby for a while. Now I love and know our son in a way that I could never have done otherwise. But I also understand the point of view of most mothers more than any other man could. When Susan gets home in the evening, I go mad with irritation if she is too tired to talk and fill me in with news of the outside world.'

Yet a father who merely takes over for the weekend while his wife retains a foothold in the adult world discovers some long-term advantages, as well as immediate insights into women's problems. By the time the children go to school, his wife will not be a drop-out from the adult world, but poised for re-entry. He will not have to suffer with her while she works through a long period of asking herself and him, 'what shall I do next?' She will probably already know.

Many men find their children more interesting once they can stand up, move around and begin to talk. But the closer the father was to his child as an infant, the earlier he developed the daily habit of playing with his child, the easier he seems to find it to develop this relationship as the child himself grows. Interrupted relationships are harder to hold together. Many a busy father looks forward to his annual holiday as a time when he can get to know his children again, but feels subtly disappointed by the experience itself once it comes. Intimacy cannot be manufactured. 'Children are not something one can pick up and put down again according to convenience, just like a book,' admits one father ruefully. 'Once you have lost touch even a little it takes a while to relax together again.' Every child and every father has interests and talents that are unique to them. Their life together is what they choose to make it. A sporty athletic father may find that he has an energetic son who loves to climb over the jungle gym with him at three, learns how to play games with him through the years, and crushingly begins to beat his father regularly on the tennis court in adolescence. But he may not. One professional athlete experienced a son who made a bee-line for the paints at the age of two, and spent the next twenty years introducing his father to the visual arts. Fathers who have the knack of getting on well with young children avoid limiting the relationships by simply indoctrinating them in their own interests and presuming that the children will follow. Instead they spread out in front of their offspring a whole range of possible things to do, and stand back and allow the children to choose what they really enjoy doing. The children soon learn to ask if they can go to the sand-pit again, they beg their father to build them a tree-house, to read a bed-time story or to tell them about what they have been doing all day. Fathers then extend the range for the children gradually. 'Whenever boredom threatens, I take my boys along to the local milk-bottling plant,' says one lawyer father. 'Both they and I get a glimpse of a very satisfying technical world.'

In families where both the parents get a chance to do plenty of things that they really like with their children there seem to be some ground rules. Father tries not to become simply the 'fun' man, while mother gets the boring chores. Sometimes the mother takes the children to a puppet show or a film, and father gets the supper ready for them when they get back. And neither mothers nor fathers allow themselves to be pressured into totally 'unisex' behaviour, always duplicating the same chores and the same treats. Children benefit from two different parents, and the parents have the right to be two different people.

One of the crucial areas that demands fathers' special awareness and contribution is their children's growing sexual development. Most parents are very aware that children as small as three years old are avidly on the look-out for clues as to their sexual identity and eager to practise the art of growing up like Mummy or like Daddy. The perpetual games of mothers and fathers, with and without dolls, the dressing up in mother's high heels and father's fishing hat, are all significant steps on the way to feeling comfortable in later years about which sex they were born to join. It is a subtle business and fathers find that they must tread gently.

No son needs a father who is anxiously watching his progress, ready to tear him away from dolls if he so much as touches his sister's cradle. Boys like dolls and teddy-bears, and are perfectly capable to playing with them in a fatherlike way. A too-anxious reaction from his father simply makes any young boy wonder why this man is fearful of him being contaminated by femininity, and produces exactly the uncertain feelings that the father wishes to prevent. Even the most expert can go astray at this point. As Dr Spock[4] has recently confessed,

> when a father makes a big issue about different playthings or chores or clothes for his son and for his daughter, this is apt to express principally his own insecurity—conscious or unconscious—about the adequacy of his maleness. I still remember when in 1936 our son, at the age of three, asked for a doll and Jane suggested buying it, with what anxious indignation I said 'No!'

Spock has now come to think that he was wrong to be so emphatic:

> Now I am convinced that though sexual identity is important, in the sense that a person should be clear and comfortable about his or her sex, emphasising differences in such matters as clothes, toys and chores is not necessary. In fact it can be detrimental. Girls and boys gain their sense of being female or male primarily from a satisfactory identification with a parent of the same sex.

Fathers who know, and show they know, which sex their children belong to find they can afford to be relaxed about the non-essential sexual trimmings. A young boy learns that he is male by finding out that he is the same as his father, who is male. He will learn to like being a male, by liking and being with that father. A young girl learns how to be a female from her similarly shaped mother. But she will learn how to be a girl who likes men, or does not trust or feel affection for men, by the way she responds to her father. The whole business of sex roles is immensely complex. While a small boy is learning how to be male from his father and from other small boys, he is learning how to be a male with a female from his mother. It is a fine line between adoring his mother across the sexual divide and feeling a rival to his father, as the healthy three-year-old does, and feeling so close to mother that he wants to grow up like her, wear her ear-rings and reject father as an alien intruder into their domestic burrow. Yet this is the line that gets criss-crossed in ways that can sometimes lead to tragedy in later years. The girl who is a 'tomboy' just tends to grow out of it; the young boy who is effeminate early may never be able to change enough. But if his father is around to transmit the unspoken knowledge that the two of them have something in common, their sex, that mother cannot join, all is well. 'Carpentry and football seem to be the two archetypal skills every young boy looks for in his father,' says Robert Andry. 'Even if father is not very good at either, his son may demand him to go through the motions.'

When father is with his children a good deal, the son learns that being a man does not involve living with both hands on the gun belt, as so much of children's television might suggest. That it is natural for men to think and read, to get angry but also to laugh and play, to be firm but also to know when to yield some ground. Some of the more crass stereotypes of masculine behaviour are only now being eradicated by fathers who refuse to pass on the strong silent tradition. 'When I was a boy it was thought rather sissy among my friends for anyone to want to read a book,' recalls one father. 'I make sure that everyone in my house feels free to relax and follow any interest. They certainly see me with a book in my hands often enough.' Father can help his son, confidently, to avoid the more extreme 'masculine' postures and allow him to believe that even aggressive fellows have feelings.

On the other hand, many fathers are beginning to be sensitive about indicating to their daughters that they are excluded from much of this masculine territory. Biologically the girl is different from father. But women suffer from a history which has defined that difference as an inferiority. Fathers now who want their daughters to grow up capable and ambitious avoid dominating them or over-protecting them. Yet children are eager to observe the real differences between the sexes, few though they may be. Among the least sex-stereotyped families, father's morning shave and mother's pregnancy are observed with fascination and a feeling of appropriateness even by the very young.

Young children between the ages of three and six are full of passionate, and sexual, emotion. Fathers get used to hearing that daughters want to marry Daddy when they grow up, and watch them try to out-flirt mother; it is during this period that young sons boil with jealousy and impotence while trying to out-do father in mother's affections. Parents who are aware of what is going on can be kinder and wiser.

When the next major crisis in the children's sexual development arrives—in adolescence—the parents often wish that some kindness could be reserved for them. Just when a man is facing the severe reassessments of middle age, his son and daughter may begin to treat him with what often looks like contempt. 'My children look on me as a buffoon', complains one suburban father. A man finds his son's capacity to outrun him on the sports field irritating, and the thought that he may soon outperform him with women fills him with dread. Fathers can experience a jealous protectiveness towards their daughters that prevents them from even pretending to be amiable to boyfriends. In some ways, the modern father's problems with his adolescents are less severe than they were. The remote, authoritarian, Victorian father had to be toppled before his son could take his place, and the bitter power conflicts that fathers and sons experienced did frequently rend the family. The father who has never been a tyrant does not have to be struck down. But his children still have to win their independence. They have to free themselves from the bonds of affection, if not from iron discipline. They may try to ignore their father, to suggest that he is out of date, to rebel against his values. Though it may often look as if they are asking him to move aside, they usually seem to feel lost if father simply abdicates. Adolescent children need father's presence even more to test themselves against. Fathers who manage to contain the storms of their children's adolescence seem to develop an attitude of initiating their children into the adult world, and welcoming them as adults, not fending them off as dreaded rivals. Many fathers find this the most difficult phase of parenthood, the period calling for the greatest effort. 'My son was so moody and angry when he was fifteen that I had to make a daily effort not to be tempted into conflict with him,' says one middle-aged father. 'But after a while he seemed to turn into a rather interesting and civilised young man.'

Effort on the children, like all effort, is repaid with added enjoyment. Curiously enough, enjoying the children seems to be mentioned most frequently at the moment by men whose marriages are splitting up. The shock of losing their children in the divorce courts, the shock of gaining them in the rare cases where mother makes it clear that she is no longer interested in parenting, seems to unfreeze masculine inhibitions and allow men to become eloquent on the pleasures of fatherhood. After a crisis they often realise how much and how little they have made of fathering so far. For Michael McFadden, who had been bringing up his three children after his wife left him, running his publishing business from home and liking it, despite crises that sometimes forced him to take a three-year-old to a business lunch, being a full-time father provided a fascinating insight into modern fathering in general. When he was met with surprise and delight by nursery school teachers who seldom ever saw another father, he reflected, 'it dawned on me that we are a society where men relinquish one of the most, if not the most vital tasks—training the children.' He took his children to visit offices where he needed to do business, because he had to. But then he began to question, 'how many fathers of teenage boys (or girls for that matter) do you know who have taken their son or daughter to the office or plant recently to watch them work? Kids in our society often grow up without any idea of what their fathers or other men do all day and consequently have trouble dealing with the real world when they enter it. This is one of the reasons that I do as much work as I can at home. My children know how I work, at least.'

As a result of his experiences as a single father, McFadden wrote his guide,[5] which is as staggering in its call on human energy as any other single-parent manual. But the reader is left with the frustrated thought that if only half that energy, and half that enthusiasm for fathering, could be aroused in a man before he was a single parent, then his wife would never feel the same need to get out and escape from her burdens. Being a single father is heroic. But it is more constructive to be half as heroic inside marriage.

What could be more baffling than the task of explaining to children the highly abstract work of the typical middle-class office worker? How many fathers get much further than saying, 'Daddy works in an office and sits at a desk all day'? But sooner or later, some part of the father's work becomes translatable into simple terms; an accountant finds he can explain why it seems important to calculate if the supermarket chain he works for should open a store in one town or in another; a salesman explains to his children what he sells and why people want it. Surveys have shown that many working-class men do not talk to their children about what they do all day because they hate their work and are ashamed of it. But that fact alone is of powerful interest to the rising generation. If men would ask for such facilities, there are few offices or factories that could not accustom themselves to let children visit occasionally and get a glimpse of the world that occupies so much of their father's time. Anything that can be presented visually strikes the most vivid sparks for the young. One architect took his five-year-old son with him on a visit to a rambling mansion that had been partially constructed a century ago and never roofed. 'I will never forget my son's face as we drove up,' he relates. 'He was wild with excitement at the incongruous sight of this beautiful building with no roof. I think he will always remember it.'

Negotiating the time to do something worth while with his children is often the most difficult part for a man. A lot of men are prisoners of their working timetables. Once they are on a professional ladder, they have the choice of climbing or getting off but not swinging free. Women have been advised for over a generation to make their career selection carefully and, in the words of one magazine article, to 'pick a job where they've heard of families'. Most women who are making anything like a success of the triple role of worker, wife and mother have heeded this advice and have been grateful for the flexibility in a law career, in medicine, or in journalism, which allowed them to run two or three clinics a week, work out legal advice from home, or write one magazine article a month while their family responsibilities were very heavy. Men as well now are beginning to give some thought to how they will balance home and work life. In the most extreme cases—such as politics—they are already aware of the conflicts that can arise. But even men who are not thinking of such pressures are beginning to anticipate some of the pitfalls ahead in combining a happy and productive life. Attitudes are changing, and so can many professional patterns.

Once men are convinced that they are making an important family contribution, they will begin to fight for more time to accomplish their paternal tasks. A number of men are already protesting that although mother is the primary parent, this has its positive aspects for father. There is an extra vision granted to the parent who is one step further away from the children. Mothers are, by instinct or learning over millions of years, experts at attachment. Fathers, by virtue of their greater distance from the children, preserve some detachment. This basic male detachment can be the foundation of much of father's contribution to family life. He begins to realise that if he looks at the family with greater objectivity than his wife can usually muster, this can be of value to his children.

In practical day-to-day terms father is often less indulgent and more demanding towards his children than their mother. And provided that the demands are sensitively tuned to the child's age and ability, this is a great benefit. Father may find himself less prepared to make excuses for an eight-year-old who cannot read, and more intent on finding some remedial methods to help him. Fathers can find their wives' permissiveness towards the children's behaviour at the table or in company profoundly irritating; they may not want to campaign for every child to sit ramrod straight as was once the fashion, but they may feel justified in asking the children to sit. Even while giving an adolescent's struggle to grow up a sympathetic understanding, father may also sense that the boy or girl appreciates being stretched mentally, and involved in setting and abiding by certain rules of behaviour. Mother may have enjoyed indulging her children with no thought of return. Father may be on hand to point out that it is healthy for the children to begin to feel that they can give as well as receive. 'We have done a lot for our children,' one father states. 'We don't want them to be on their knees in gratitude. But they should understand that care and concern are a two-way thing.'

The fact that father's discipline has so often been over-rigid or apathetic does not invalidate the idea that father, because he is not mother, can be especially effective in setting limits to what the children may do. Many small children who are still intensely involved with their mothers find it almost unbearable to accept that the same parent who smiles on them, also frowns; that the mother who binds up their wounds, also smacks. Many mothers who would like to insist on certain minimum standards simply get worn down until they overlook anything and everything their children do. If father is there to step in gently but firmly, everyone's face can be saved. 'The children know that their father will not stand their being rude and cheeky to me,' says one mother, 'and I am grateful that he is able to interfere and prevent every argument from becoming a slanging match.'

Discipline can be most effectively applied by someone who has learned some of the basic facts of instructing children. 'They are asking for a smacking', is many a father's reaction if the boys are jumping all over the furniture. In fact, the children are asking to be taught the difference between the climbing-frame in the garden and the chairs in the house. To teach a child to behave in such a way that other people find him pleasant to live with takes time. It also takes method. Men can use their children's insistent longing for father's attention to reinforce the kind of behaviour they want to promote. When a two-year-old learns to use a spoon well, when a ten-year-old finishes his homework with every sign of brisk enjoyment, the father makes an impression if he then steps in with praise. After a bout of infantile naughtiness or adolescent rebellion, a curt brief sign of disapproval offers the child the minimum of disappointed attention. By and large, children are prepared to abandon or question activities that make father turn away and ignore them. Encouragement works like a charm in supervising studies also. 'There wasn't too much that I could find to praise my son for when he started school,' says one father. 'He seemed to do hardly anything well. But I tried hard to pick out a subject where he was making headway, or a teacher that he had made an impression on. Gradually he started to put more effort into his work and I think now that he is beginning to be quite proud of himself.'

Most children can be brought to see that it is in their best interests to co-operate if adults are reasonable in their demands. And most children can be forced to understand that adults have rights as well as responsibilities. As the less indulgent member of the parental team, father sticks up for some of the rights of parents. Though the child-centred and permissive house may be the greatest benefit for under-school-age children, as the family grows up, the system shifts; parents spend less time adapting to a baby's needs and more time getting a ten-year-old to adapt to adult standards such as cleanliness. Parents begin to insist on times of day when they would like some peace and privacy, on special rooms in the house where toys and children's books should not take over. Any couple benefits from time to time by getting away, by leaving the children with grandparents or close friends while they take a much needed short holiday. Husbands often take the initiative in organising ways for themselves and their wives to survive the devouring instincts of children. Fathers are often the first to notice that the children are wielding too much power, and that the house is run too much for them.

Though fathers read fewer books on child care than mothers, this can even be an advantage. Bringing up children is a highly individual and personal affair. If one parent is not aware of all the latest fashionable trends in child upbringing, he can counterbalance the other who may too easily fall victim to the prevailing propaganda. Twenty years ago, child psychologists were laying special stress on the needs of children to adapt to their peers. Today they are beginning to have doubts about the overriding influence of the peer-group and to protest that children do not spend enough time with adults. Father may not be aware of these shifting views. But he may have always had a common-sense conviction that young Johnny should not spend all his time milling around with other seven-year-olds but go fishing on Saturdays with him. Some undiluted adult influence, some times each day and each week when the child can be alone with his father and able to talk with him, and able to check the frequently nonsensical beliefs of children against his greater knowledge, give the two generations a chance to understand each other's ideas and values, and spin a continuous web of civilisation.

If a father starts early to take an interest in the books and television programmes, the games and crazes of his children's age-group—and the child's cultural milieu shifts very rapidly— he can also make sure that his children begin to learn from the beginning about what interests him, the music and books and sports that a grown-up prefers. From the beginning, children need to learn that adults have acquired wisdom and culture and interests and that they can be initiated into their meaning. Keeping the balance right between the demands of the children's generation and the inheritance from father's is tricky. In a number of families in the past, the younger generation never did get a chance to avoid the values of the old and make their own world. Today, the situation is reversed and many young people seem never to have had indicated to them that the world existed before they were born. 'Father must tune in to the needs of the next generation, but not sell out to the peer group,' says Robert Andry. 'He needs to build bridges between them and his own traditional values.' If father can manage it, as the children grow up the generations are enriched by each other's knowledge and ways of seeing the world, not divided by a gap.

Mother's increasing influence and father's decline has involved some losses. Mother's indulgence to her children can be immensely beneficial, especially in the early years. But it also has its drawbacks. One of the most obvious is that, if the mother continues for too long to surround the child with a blissful, protected atmosphere, the child will never be able to face up as an adult to the many horrors of real life. It is kinder to a child to let reality in gradually; to expect courage and stamina from ten-year-olds, and not allow an individual to face his first tough situation at the age of twenty-five. As one psychologist says, 'a great deal of adult neurosis is caused by an over-indulgent upbringing, where the children have never been allowed to find out how horrible the real world can be; adult life then comes as too much of a shock.' Some of the current search for 'total fulfilment', for the realisation of 'full human potential', can seem like the quest of spoiled children who cannot believe that they are going to be denied anything by life, who want it all and want it now. A certain stoicism, patience and gratitude for what they do get are character traits that can make for greater happiness. But these are not aspects of character that are easily acquired by the over-indulged. As Abraham Maslow has written, 'the demand for "Nirvana now" is itself a major source of evil.'[6]

If father is in his rightful place, and ready and willing to temper mother's indulgence by making some demands of his own, the children will be given the benefit of adapting to different kinds of reality. Mother's attitude to childhood can be 'gather ye rosebuds while ye may'; father may see childhood as a training camp. Both views offer some, but different, benefits. In their future life as adults, they will have a chance to find out that mother's capacity for pleasure, sympathy and intimacy has bred them to make some of the right emotional choices, and to lead a vivid personal life; but that the less indulgent attitude of their father has taught them how to expect effort from themselves, in standards of work and of achievement, in patience to set their sights on long-term goals. Mother, ideally, teaches the children that they matter enormously, because they matter to her; father is ideally placed to teach them that there are other people and other things that matter as well.

That mother and father balance each other, mitigate each other's influence, and broaden the emotional and mental range, seems obvious. Children benefit from having a number of significant and different adults in their lives; grandparents, uncles and aunts, and friends. But at the very least, two adults involved in their upbringing can counteract each other's more bizarre tendencies, and complement each other's talents and blind spots. In the broadest sense, fathers provide their children with a second opinion on life. And in many different phases, they can offer to remedy the excesses of mothers. Some women wait on their children for years and prevent them from ever learning to look after themselves. Father may need to step in firmly and insist that the children are forced to be more independent. In adolescence he may have to start the long process of untying mother's apron-strings, and preparing her and the children for the separations that college and work may bring. And, in some cases, father can have a vital part to play in diagnosing the point at which mother's nervous or mental disabilities have reached a stage where the children are noticeably suffering, and some outside intervention is needed. It may be that father will be the one to develop emotional or mental problems. But statistically it is more likely to be mother. The pressures on her at the moment are more severe; and because her relationship with the children is still closer, her mental state will have the greatest effect on the children.

'At the point where I got a promotion and we had to lead a more demanding social life, we also moved house and lived among builders' rubble for months, and Penny was just starting back into teaching. Very naturally, life became too much for her', says one alert husband. 'We got through a very difficult period only when I arranged plenty of help from Penny's mother, a more understanding attitude from the new schools where the children were starting, and finally a damn good holiday for the two of us, that gave us a chance to come to life again.' Heading everyone away from a breakdown by this kind of active intervention is a crucial task for any involved adult. If father is the one who is intelligent and aware enough to spot the trouble and help to solve it, he will have saved his family just as surely as if he had rescued them from starvation in an earlier age.

The problem is not that there is nothing left any more for father to do. There is so much for him to do, but he has to work out for himself what it is that is needed. It is less easy than the old predictable Victorian role. But a lot more interesting. He does not have to be odd man out in the modern family, but has to work at being odd man in. He has the luxury of writing his own scenario, of inventing his own ideas of how an intelligent and capable man lives with and helps his wife and children. Having and rearing children is one of the most significant and enriching achievements of a man's life as well as of a woman's. Many men today are beginning to realise that women have traditionally made their children important, not simply from no alternative, not simply from altruism, but from a very sure sense of where one of the greatest satisfactions in living can lie. In his last novel, *Islands in the Stream*, Ernest Hemingway's dogged (and recognisable) painter hero reflects back over his chequered love-life and assesses that 'he had been able to replace almost everything, except the children, with work.'

Children also judge their father's contribution as highly influential on their lives. The compliments they pay may be oblique. Young writer Martin Amis recalls of his divorced father, Kingsley Amis, 'I was always very good at English. My father took a silent interest and held off. It's difficult to distinguish between tact and real torpor.' Or they may be effusive. 'My father taught me how to work,' says one appreciative country doctor. 'I learned from seeing him on call at all hours, exhausted but pleased to be needed. I was determined to have the same kind of life.'

To make so many adjustments to marriage and fatherhood may appear difficult to many men, and downright impossible to some. Many may wonder why on earth they should bother. Why should father have to be so co-operative and considerate? He has frequently managed to avoid being so in the past. But the past is over. Father no longer has a monopoly on providing for his family; both parents now share in that. 'And if I am not the great provider, what am I?', asks one of today's fathers. He may well ask. As father's economic source of power in the family declines, so he needs to substitute other skills, or lose influence altogether. The contribution that can earn him a continuing and honoured position is that of personal skill, and thoughtful involvement in how the family is run. If father does not want to take on this kind of responsibility, the future is bleak, for the family but especially for him. One of the effects of democratic modes of thinking is that the old chasms between power and responsibility are disappearing. Power now tends to go to those who assume the responsibility, in politics, in industry, in the family. And because mother is taking the family responsibility, she is gaining the power. A thoughtful modern father does not have to let that happen.

If a man can find a way to enjoy, as well as work at, the task of bringing up his offspring, he will not only make his own life more satisfying but guarantee satisfactions ahead for his children. The next generation can sign a new treaty to call a halt to the sex-war only if father helps them now. His participation is needed for both sexes to grow up with an equal appreciation of fathers and mothers, without undue resentments towards men or towards women. Sexism can only finally be routed in the family. As one psychologist has said, 'the biggest deprivation children suffer is not having been enjoyed by both parents.' It is now time to set this right. Father's place is in the home.

NINE FATHERING THE Mixed Family

Over the last two decades, a number of variations on the theme of fatherhood have begun to be worked out. Impermanent marriage, and a permissive attitude to couples who live together outside marriage, is transforming many aspects of the paternal role. In the future, the majority of men may still choose to live with one woman of their own generation and produce with her 2.5 children, but a number of minorities are already demonstrating alternative paternity. In many cases, men start another marriage with a younger wife and a new family in middle age, and live to confront a new brood of adolescents across a two-generation gap in old age. In other instances, men are found today living with the woman of their choice and that woman's children. 'Father' in a number of families means what it does to the New Guinea islander, 'the man who lives with mother'. Occasionally if father is one of those rare men who have won custody and day-to-day care of their children after divorce, he may find himself later sitting round the family table with his second wife and children who are, in blood terms, 'one of mine, two of yours, and one of ours'.

If fathering is increasingly a matter of feeling rather than feeding, then father can direct his paternal interest where he wishes. To some children, perhaps his own in blood, he may be forced to be only a Sunday afternoon father; for others, possibly his children only through his choice of their mother as his living companion, he may be engaged in the daily chores of tying shoelaces and dropping them off to their swimming class.

One of father's most crucial problems in the future may turn out to be how well he copes with the role of step-father. And one of the calculations men must make collectively is whether the final vestige of their traditional authority is ceded by becoming step-father instead of father.

The name step-father is no help to any man. In the past, the very word carried with it a ring of doom. From infancy, fairy-tales with all their haunting potency gave us ideas of what horrors step-parents were capable of. Though a number of exceptional men have always been able to develop feelings of affection for children who were not bound to them by any blood tie, the whole network of patriarchy was designed to encourage a man to feel mainly resentment towards any son or daughter who was not his offspring. When father's breadwinning role was crucial to survival, and he alone undertook the burden of producing the family income, he might have been justified in objecting to having children who were not his foisted upon him. When father was so greatly involved with his son as an heir, as someone to carry on the family name, the blood tie was of over-riding importance. Today, two incomes in the majority of families divide the worry of providing for the children. And the blood tie is less worshipped than before. Recent investigations into adoption have shown how very effective adoptive parents are, and demonstrated that children benefit from parents who made a conscious decision to undertake parenting.[1] Commitment is everything; when that is present, the blood tie can become almost irrelevant. And parents' attitudes to their children have changed immeasureably in this century. Today, parenthood has fewer overtones of ownership than ever. The rights of children are of paramount concern to all those seriously concerned with the family. And the adults who now make the decision to become parents are looking for satisfactions in living with children that many middle-class parents in the past knew nothing about; these are the existential pleasures of shared experiences and intimate feelings. Individuals today look for the emotional rewards of being parents to their children, just as they look for emotional rewards from being husbands and wives.

For all these reasons, the path to enjoying the company of a child because that child is part of a loved adult is smoother than ever before. But what problems are inherent in the role of step-father? What real weight does a man carry in a family where he is an adopted parent? What family unity can he symbolise if only half the children are his in blood? How skilful does he have to be, if he arrives late in a child's life, and gets to know the child first as an adjunct of the mother, to come to feel intimately involved with that child? Can he ever develop as secure and permanent a bond with a step-child as with a child of his own? And if he cannot, what is the real contribution of the adopted father?

When two divorced adults come together and marry, and bring with them to their new life children from their first marriages, the problems of welding together her children, who most probably still live with their mother, and his children, who most probably only visit father, are obviously enormous. In a re-marriage, as in any new partnership, the two adults are learning to relax and trust another individual again. Some of the children have to learn to trust and accept a new man in the family, and share mother with him, when the previous man they shared her with may have shown how much he appreciated their generosity by walking out. Other children have to accept seeing their father as permanent protector not of their mother, but of a new woman. The resident children may have to accept step-brothers and step-sisters who arrive at weekends to prodigal-son type receptions and stir feelings of competition and resentment. Cliques and unexpected alliances may threaten the formation of a unified family group. In any family, the firstborn child experiences some emotional problems in welcoming the new baby. And, Lucile Duberman suggests,[2] in a mixed family 'there are two "first born children", which doubles the likelihood and intensity of disorder.' Father may take some years working out what are his rights and his obligations in this new unit; his first overtures of friendship may be rebuffed, particularly if the children feel that he is trying to replace their own father. The step-father may have to endure a period when he is being tested out by the children to see how far he can be pushed; his intention to lie low at first and give the children time to adjust may be interpreted by them as a sign of weakness and he will have to work out exactly where and when he must assert himself. Father will also have to cope with the wider relations, such as a mother-in-law who liked the first partner more. 'The main problem for the step-father is the step-family,' complains one combatant.

The essential character of his part is disguised, not clarified, by the terms. 'Step-father' is a name that lingers on from past centuries when fathers died and the family looked about for a necessary replacement. Another father stepped into the dead father's role. But the new man who joins any woman and her children after a divorce is not a replacement; he is an additional parent. He does not try to oust the first father, but to supplement his efforts. The step-parent relationship is too often denied its special character, claims Paul Bohannan,[3] either by an attempt to pretend that there can be no real relationship between a new spouse and children of a previous marriage, or by an effort to pretend that the step-parent relationship is exactly the same as any other kind of parenting. Yet a supplementary father, in an age of diminished fathering, can have a beneficial role to play.

And some name is necessary for such an important new arrival in the family. The ever-recurring query, 'what shall I call him?' is usually resolved by the children calling their step-father by his first name. Most parents agree that only one man has a right to be 'Daddy', the biological father. This makes the father-in-residence a first-name pal; but it can also curiously underline that he is a man in search of a role. Sometimes children desperately feel the need for another title for the man of the family. When one young Londoner was approached by a child in his school, and asked, with some sophistication, 'what do you call the man in your house?' the boy returned home and asked his mother, 'although I can't call him "Daddy" because I see my Daddy at weekends, please may I call Tony "step-father" when there are other children here so that they will know who he is?' Children who suffer from a biological father who never turns up to see them from one year to the next begin to show their needs by referring pointedly to their resident step-father as 'my dad' among their friends.

Part of the step-father's role, like the father's, is just being there, symbolising that there is a male who is interested in the family welfare. And for this reason, a number of sociologists have suggested that it is much easier for a man to make a success of step-fathering than it is for any woman to make a success of being anyone's step-mother. In the nature of the present custody laws, women do not have to make the attempt so often, but when they do they are grappling with very primitive feelings in themselves and in the children. Just how bitter the emotional atmosphere can get has been revealed by journalist and step-parent Brenda Maddox in *The Half-Parent*. In so far as any step-father does not seek out too demanding a part for himself in the family, but is content to remain fairly passive, he may be able to coast without incurring too much resentment from anyone. 'The step-father's advantage is the nature of the father's role,' writes Leonard Benson.[4] 'It is not as demanding as the maternal role.'

But if a modern step-father sees his role differently and tries to do something more than simply live passively in the background, what are the hazards he faces? The emotional conflicts for any man who has to accept that his own children will only be weekly visitors, while his wife's children will be permanent residents, can be severe. His ability to play a full paternal role may be diminished towards both sets of children. He most probably will not have full legal custody of either family. To his own children, he can only be a part-time father, a weekend influence, an intermittent friend. To his wife's children, he is a courtesy extra parent, an adult who can at best perhaps be a benevolent uncle, at worst an interloper who arouses their jealousy. One step-father says:

> I find that I can get through the working week fairly easily, although I miss my children and sometimes get a little irritable trying to cope with Christine's two girls. But at weekends the resentments really start to show. I want to see my children, but if I take Christine along, they don't make her feel very welcome. And if I stay with Christine and the girls, her children sometimes let me realise that they don't always want to be sharing their mother with me. We are just beginning to try to have all of the children at the house together, for short holidays. They seem to get interested in working out how to react to each other then, and some of the conflicts get diverted from Christine and me.

In a study of a number of 'reconstituted families', as sociologists like to call them, Charles Bowerman and Donald Irish reported that, in all kinds of families, the children generally feel more affection for the mothers than for the fathers, but that in families with a step-father, 'the level of affection towards step-father is usually markedly lower than towards real fathers. Thus the *difference* in attitudes towards parents is greater in this type of step-home than in homes containing both real parents.'[5] In other words, step-father, even when he is making an effort to make a good job of it, is the parent who is less regarded. He is the parent once removed, and the intense emotional loyalty towards the mother is shown up in even stronger contrast.

Any step-father has to exercise the greatest tact in trying to overcome the difficulties inherent in his position. Children are very quick to recognise when an adult wants to manipulate them, and any intensive campaign to win their co-operation usually seems to do more harm than good. But children seldom reject genuine friendship that is tactfully offered. And the one certain factor that can be made to work to help the step-father is the devotion that the children feel towards their mother. If their step-father over the years makes their mother's life happier than it was with her first husband, they will also benefit from the greater harmony, and they will notice their debt to their step-father. A number of men in this situation have managed to reverse the usual pessimistic predictions. One mother quoted by Lucile Duberman[6] had this to say of her husband's relationship to her child: 'He's always referred to her as his daughter rather than as his step-daughter. He never made any issue of her being a step-child. There are times when I think she is closer to him than she is to me. He is more her father than her real father ever was or is now.'

Most of the interest that professional investigators have displayed for 'reconstituted families' has been focused on the problems that children have in coping with the changes in their family life. Child adjustment is their greatest preoccupation. Father adjustment is overlooked. Yet the roundabout route to step-fatherhood is full of emotional hurdles.

A young step-father, David Herbert, says:

When I first met Marianne, I frankly don't remember taking very much notice of Christopher. Of course, I knew she was separated from her husband and had a three-year-old son. But I just patted him on the head, and he gave me measles and there was not much more to it. But as I got more and more fond of Marianne I found myself disliking Christopher. I used to rationalise this and say that it was because he was an impediment to our relationship. But in fact I really did not like him. I thought that he was rather effeminate; he was living at home with his mother and grandmother and he may have been. Of course, Marianne found my opinion very hard to take and so did her mother. But there it was. There was a long period when I had to decide what to do. Marianne was waiting for a divorce. We would have moved in together very quickly if we had not had to consider Christopher. But we did not want to inflict any more instability on him. I had to think hard and ask myself how I would react to Christopher over the years. What would I think of him when he was a boy of twelve, or a young man of twenty? Eventually I said to myself: 'I want to marry Marianne and Christopher is part and parcel of it. I want to look after them both.'

After Marianne and I began to live together, I was very careful not to make any special overtures to Christopher. I did not deliberately work at a relationship with him. I just let it develop. The dislike disappeared as I got to know and understand him better. Some of the things that had irritated me before about him either did not seem to matter any more, or I found that they irritated his mother equally. My own father was very helpful. I waited a while before presenting Marianne and Christopher to him, but he accepted it all straight away. He is very good with children, and he told me that I could be a help to Christopher. Marianne does not always feel that she gets total backing from me in matters of discipline. Perhaps she and I see my role a little differently. I am slow to chastise. But I think it has worked out very well. Christopher calls me 'David' at home, but 'my dad' to his friends. I think of him as my son. Jack, his natural father, made a surprise visit once when the boy was five. Christopher had no recollection of him at all, and Jack simply announced his identity. I was very angry on Christopher's behalf. It was such an irresponsible thing to do. But he never reappears. A few years ago, Christopher said on his birthday, 'I won't get anything from Jack because you can't rely on him.' That was the child's own conclusion. But Jack's graceful fading out has been a great help to me.

Christopher is an independent child, self-sufficient. He keeps his distance, and this has made my involvement with him not too intense. I take him running on Sunday mornings, but a lot of the time he is doing his homework, and I am preoccupied . . . I never thought of myself as the very fatherly type. And I was quite content to have just one child. To be frank, I always thought I was lucky to have missed out on the nappies and the messy bit. But Marianne wanted another baby. So two years ago our daughter was born. And it was a revelation to me. I saw her born and that was the most fantastic experience. The doctors very skilfully involved me; they made me hold the oxygen mask and help generally. And the first two years of her life have been marvellous for me. I haven't minded the nappies, I don't mind what I do for her. But I now have two entirely separate sets of emotions. I don't feel as protective towards Christopher as I do towards her. If Christopher is half an hour late, I don't worry. But I think that if she is ever half an hour late I shall go berserk. I feel guilty at times about my excess of affection for her. Is he going to turn round to me one day and say, 'You only care about that little girl'? In fact Christopher adores her. Because he is so much older he is quite fatherly to her. He will never let a baby-sitter do anything for her; he insists on changing her nappies and finding her toys. And because both children require such different attention from us, he with his homework and she with her feeding, they don't compete. But now my whole life is so different. I'm a convert. I'm just so pro fatherhood.

Almost inevitably, the mixed family lives with some very mixed feelings, no matter how fairly each member tries to distribute affections and obligations. But there is some evidence that step-relationships have in the past been awarded an undeservedly bad press. Given the will to succeed, many re-marriages provide a better life for all the family members than anything they had known before. After surveying a sample of eighty-eight 'reconstituted' families in the United States to examine the relations between the step-parents and step-children, and between step-siblings, Lucile Duberman[7] found that 78 per cent of the group rated themselves 'excellent' in their adjustment to each other, and she concluded that 'in general, the step-parent step-child relationship was a reasonably good one, much better than most previous research has found.'

Given the necessary good will, many difficult family situations can be turned to advantage, and step-fatherhood can obviously be one of them. A step-father can learn to make his lesser emotional involvement with his wife's children a greater benefit than the influence of many natural fathers ever is. Like mother's husband in the Trobriand Islands, step-father may find himself freer to express a lot of friendly affection when he is quite clear that he is not called on to be any kind of authority figure. There is less temptation for a step-father to put pressure on the children to excel and reflect glory on him; step-father's ego is much less involved. There is more opportunity for a less intense but very enjoyable friendship to evolve. Children can learn about masculine affection and masculine interests from a step-father as well as from a natural father, and the model that a step-father provides may be beneficial because it is less threatening and less powerful than the image of father himself. The step-father's affection and interest undoubtedly differ from that of the mother, in that he cannot be presumed to be as partial and indulgent as she is. But there can be many advantages for the children once they are willing to work to gain his approval.

Yet in the web of relationships inside the mixed family, father is obviously only one of the leaders, one of the contenders for attention. Four parents at least may be involved, with varied claims to authority over the lives of the children. The resident father cannot with any great security rely on a united response to any appeal that he makes. Step-father has to be very careful not to overplay his hand. Sections of the family can rule themselves like semi-autonomous states inside a union. Perhaps this is the democratic family par excellence. As such, it seems to appeal to many of the children who grow up in it. 'What the children seem to like about it,' says one mother of a large mixed family, 'is that this is the nearest thing to a commune.'

One father who manages to negotiate the rapids of his multiple obligations with skill is Robert Waring and his second wife, Jane, who live in Surrey. Jane and Robert and their first spouses were all friends before their split, but over the years it became obvious that Jane's husband was nearly always away working and found it hard to remember that he had three children, and Robert's wife was nearly always off to a party and found it boring to remember that she had two daughters. Jane and Robert found that they were the pair who were left talking over and enjoying such topics as the local schools or new children's books, one son's inability to play basketball, a daughter's bad marks for French. After about eight years of this, they decided that they would rather be married to each other. Despite bitter custody disputes with their first partners—Robert's wife was awarded custody of their children but when it came down to it she decided to trade them for other benefits—the children finally all ended up living with the parents who had always done the parenting. To their already substantial family, Jane and Robert added a final young son, a 'mutual' child to cement the family; Robert found himself living with six children who all meant different things to him, and who all looked on him in very different ways.

Robert describes himself as 'a very domestic animal', not in the sense that he likes to paint shelves or dig up the garden, but in that he likes to get a lot of his interest and pleasure from his home. His young son has set the seal on his life.

> Alan has put another peak into life. I find that with him I am more affectionate that I thought I could be with any child, very physically affectionate. Now that I've got Alan it has supplied a feeling of satisfaction. I have a greater ambition, and in a lot of things I try harder. He is at the age now where he regards me as infallible. I have to remember that. Even if I want to be, I can't be diffident and easy-going.

As a parent, Robert differs from his wife, he says, because 'I can discipline more severely and spoil more severely. I go to extremes. She keeps up the stable, middle way. I shout louder, and spend more.' When Robert was still living with his first wife, he was always the one to get up early on a weekend morning, even if he had been working late the night before, to take the girls to their riding lessons. 'I enjoyed giving them something to do,' he recalls. 'I accept that you narrow your life when you have young children, but if you don't introduce them to these outlets when they are small, they won't be interested in them later.'

Adjusting to his step-children as well, although he had known them as a family friend for many years, took some time and effort. 'At first, I found it very difficult not to show stronger feelings for some of the children. Things got easier when I abandoned the effort to be so fair and just let myself slip back into an "uncle" role with my step-children for a while. Now, after six years, it has evened out and it is a much easier relationship with all of them.'

One of the key areas of tension is the attempt, no matter how tactful, at discipline, at any obvious exercise of authority.

In the beginning, in the first three years, I found it very difficult to tell Jane's children what to do. I was also very conscious of their own father living quite near by. And one of Jane's children, the boy who was then seven, was in a very protective mood towards his mother, and he was looking for a confrontation. After he provoked me to a real fight one day we got on a little better. But I think that I am still more tactful about telling Jane's children to do things; I am liable to tell Jane to tell them to do things. And Jane's way of bringing them up anyway has been a little different from mine. I can be more strict and I can be more soft.

There are still plenty of problems. Both parents confess that 'the character traits of the other parents, when they turn up in the children, are very irritating. We try not to be irritated, but it is impossible not to react. But we never indulge in ancestor buck-passing; we don't accuse a child of being "just like your father"!' With such a large, spaced-out family, Robert feels that, economically, he is on a treadmill, and is worried that this earning power may decline before his young son is through with his education. Jane realises that she has been going to PTA meetings for fifteen years already, and will not be finished for another fifteen. But both agree that the last baby cemented the family. Says Jane, 'to each of us he means something different—a first son for my husband, a last child for me.' And Jane stresses that it is partly Robert's paternal talent that has made their composite family work successfully. 'Robert is just a terribly fair man; he treats children like people. And he doesn't expect his life to be separate from them, he enjoys living with them.'

No one in such a family pretends that the members have not picked up some scars on the way to their final happiness and stability. But many mixed families are certain that their present life is more harmonious and productive than anything that has gone before. In many ways it strikes the observer as an ideal contemporary compromise; flexible, tolerant, democratic. But it is hard to escape the conclusion that this is still one more family situation in which mother's hand is strengthened and father's is made more uncertain. Step-father in general seems to display the modern father role at its most tentative. The part of step-father allows any man to exercise his skills in family diplomacy, to head off explosive situations with some delicacy and tact, to lead subtly from behind. But how easy is it for step-father ever to lead from in front? For him even to attempt to do so might expose and crack open the seams where the family has been joined. Neither legally, nor economically, does he exercise any final control. Whereas the modern father in his first marriage can often earn for himself the position of first among equals, the step-father's position is very equal indeed. As one frustrated step-parent admits, 'even negotiating to get every interested party to agree to where and when the combined family holiday is going to be can be amazingly difficult.'

The increasing number of re-marriages and resulting mixed families will force the step-father role upon many men who may not have suspected before that such emotional demands might be made upon them, and such severe limits set to their power to exercise their responsibilities. Father's place may be in the home. But does he really want his home to be turned into a commune?

TEN The Future for Father

A redefinition of fatherhood seems to be an essential piece in solving the sex-puzzle. Men as well as women need to invent their roles anew. As things stand at the moment, many men feel that they have not grasped what is required of them in the family setting; their women and children are disappointed that father's uncertainty so often makes him back away from any close involvement in their lives.

Hardly anyone thinks that father is doing a grand job. A public opinion poll[1] conducted among teenagers to find out who was the figure that they most admired found that 'mother' overwhelmingly took first place (followed by the Queen). Father came fifth. Gratitude to father seems to come a long way after similar feelings for mother in any nation's consciousness. Though 'Mother's Day' has been part of the US government's recognised calendar since 1914, it was only in 1972 that the Americans assigned a special day to Father.

Some forecasters, of course, think that instead of bending our thoughts to re-inventing father, we should be bracing ourselves to say a final 'goodbye'. There are those who envision a future in which father has been replaced by a sperm bank, and teenage girls queue to be impregnated with the heroic seed of their choice—perhaps choosing to perpetuate a line of Dr Kissingers or Mick Jaggers, according to their whim. Other prophets have pondered the idea of turning over care and responsibility for the children entirely to mothers, and compensating them by taxing all males in the population heavily to provide a sort of mothers' pension. How men would feel about such an abstract providing role is not clear. But many quite sober futurologists seem to assume that we can look forward to a further abandonment of fatherhood; that father is going to continue to be too busy, too shell-shocked after divorce or too uninterested to play much of a part in raising his children. They take for granted that the increasing range of choices open to adults on how they live and with whom they live and according to what ideals they live will seldom include a decision by a man and a woman to stay together to rear their offspring, and integrate their love, work and marriage into one family whole. A psychologist like Carl Levett,[2] seeking solutions to the problems raised by father's further retirement from the family scene and ways for him to avoid the accusation 'you don't spend enough time with your son', has hit on the idea of a 'third parent' to be allotted to each busy family, a sort of resident Boy Scout specifically trained to be a father-substitute. 'With paternal figures in diminishing supply,' writes Levett, 'greater use will need to be made of supplementary masculine resources to close the father-son guidance gap.'

Of course, families have incorporated 'third' parents in the past. The dedicated English nanny was such a one, and she released the nineteenth-century upper classes for the cares of Empire or the social whirl, and at the same time gave to whole generations of British children an unshakeable personal stability bordering on arrogance, which made them a byword around the world. Nannies generally stayed throughout the entire childhood of their charges, and effectively shielded the children from many stresses, including those produced by the unhappy marriages of their parents. Jonathan Gathorne-Hardy relates in *The Rise and Fall of the British Nanny* the story of one small child who overhead shouts and abuse from his parents' bedroom and worriedly asked nanny what was the matter. 'Mummy and Daddy are rehearsing a play,' he was told, and anxiety was smoothed away. 'The rehearsals went on for years,' the author adds.

But nanny was not only a permanent figure; unlike modern helps to parents, she was of greater age and lesser social status. She posed no sexual threat. A 'third parent' now might be more disruptive. What a second male around the house might do today is anybody's guess. Today's parents also want to be intimate with their children. They hope to get pleasure out of knowing them. They do not turn readily to the nanny-figures or the boarding school which both take over the parental role. A 'third parent' to help father might add to, rather than subtract from paternal guilt. It must be, and perhaps always was, the preposterous and expensive nature of most of the alternatives that have driven humanity back again and again to the relatively workable unit of the traditional family.

The two-parent family is doubtless going to continue to prove that it has far from outlived its usefulness for a long time yet. And once the basic problems of father's role have been pinpointed and analysed, solutions that will help him, and therefore every member of the family, can be looked for. The old stereotype of father, a figure of terrible power, has faded. The notion of father as the natural symbol of authority may sound about as relevant to us as the theory of the Divine Right of Kings; today authority has to be earned. And there lies the crucial change for father. In past centuries when his symbolic authority as head of the family was unquestioned, distance, a certain apartness from the day-to-day intimacies of family life, lent more awe to father's position.[3] When father was the sole munificent provider, his preoccupation in dealing with the great affairs of the world made him more impressive. But now we all earn our own equal authority. We all, to a greater or lesser extent, deal with affairs outside the family. The old patriarchal mystique has therefore gone, and the apartness, the certain distance that once helped father to deal with his family, now spells disaster for him. Involvement today becomes the key to father's position in the family. This is the reason why father must be encouraged to find work and play some of his time within the family setting. Not primarily to ease mother's burdens, but to construct a place for himself, to ensure that he is seen to be needed.

Men who have not yet grasped this basic switch—from paternal detachment to paternal involvement—are frequently bewildered and saddened to find their personal lives in ruins. That work outside the family does not automatically provoke appreciation inside the family comes as a nasty surprise. 'Many men believe that their devotion to the job will bring them love,' writes the American author Warren Farrell,[4] 'but find it has instead alienated them from those they love. This situation embitters many men, since they have invested their lives and status in something they expected would bring affection.'

It is in no one's best interests to let men fail in family life. Men, first of all, need to find their children satisfying, to be stabilised themselves by the demands of the generation who look to them for guidance and who will follow them. Masculine uncertainty today is as much due to the fact that many men are ill at ease with their children, as to the difficulties that they have in recognising the aims of their wives. Men need women, but they also need their children more than they have ever been allowed to know. Men have been indoctrinated in the past with the idea that women are vulnerable and need a partner throughout life; they have been partly taught that children need a male protector. What has seldom been openly expressed and accepted is that men also need to be fathers. Yet the family role is highly beneficial to men. Marriage and fatherhood make men physically and emotionally healthier, as Jessie Bernard has shown in *The Future of Marriage*. It is not therefore safe to allow a social pattern to emerge which leaves too many disconnected, unhappy males. A man with 'no family ties' may be the ideal mobile cog in the business machine, but he is also the prime candidate for illness, depression and suicide. Fatherhood gives a man a place where he belongs, interests in the present, and hopes and plans for the future. Fatherhood helps to overcome masculine detachment and makes the man a member of a domestic team; it supports the uncertain masculine ego and gives him a source of pride; it provokes him to use his energies by giving him a motive and harnesses them to socially useful goals.

A father can also learn from his children, and can be matured by them. Women have been learning from children for years; where else did they get their acute sense of personal psychology that used to be coyly referred to as 'intuition'? One of the first things a father learns from his children is that his needs can match theirs. They look to him for instruction; he can enjoy giving instruction. The children look to him as a model, and being a model adds an extra dimension to his decisions. His ambitions and achievements look different to him if he can learn to look at them through their eyes as well as his own. The constant discovery of how different and how similar he is to his wife is reflected with interesting variations in his son and daughter.

Men need to get a little nervous about what is happening to marriage. Instead of looking at the short-term sexual advantages of the present fluid situation, they need to become more aware of the possible long-term losses. They have to go back to the old anthropological law; if men want to be fathers they have to be husbands. The burden of working out new systems of marriage and the family, new roles that will not make women feel as frustrated as they do today, falls as squarely on men as on women. They have to understand what is happening to female psychology. The old textbook view of feminine mentality as passive and accepting was the psychology not of women but of pregnant women; such acceptance was the ultimate in adaptation to their situation in life. But women are no longer pregnant every year, so they are different creatures. Their health and freedom to manoeuvre has altered the terms of marriage. In the past, dominance was the price that men extracted for taking on the task of feeding their perpetually pregnant wives and growing brood of children. Today, mother and children are beginning to charge father an entrance fee for admission to the family; co-operation. And he needs to pay it. Father may have become less important to the family but the family is now becoming more important to him.

Such a conclusion suggests to some that women have now become the dominant sex, and that roles are so far reversed that men must seek their fulfilment in keeping women happy in marriage and ministering to all their needs, as women once used to do for men. At the end of a witty, anguished discussion of current masculine problems in search of fatherhood, the American novelist Stephen Koch wryly concludes: 'feminism's vision of "equal human beings" blandly assumes the steady continuation of happy fulfilled satisfying marriage, in which there is to be a male role after all; it is to be a *totally accommodating husband*.'[5] But perhaps a truer definition would be that women hope men can be as accommodating in marriage as women have generally been, as aware of what they have to lose as women are. Says psychologist James Hemmings:

> There is no way forward except through equality, but it is
> important that women do not push men too far. At the
> moment, men do not as a general rule fight women
> physically and beat them up. But this is a magnanimity
> that asserted itself at some point in social evolution. Some

point was reached when men presumably realised that they could achieve more with women by not beating them up. A similar magnanimity is necessary now from women, so that women do not push men under psychologically.

The modern world has already deprived men of many facets of their lives. They have lost their wider kin, the cousins, uncles and innumerable brothers who used to help them towards a sense of belonging. At each loss they have filled the vacuum with yet more work. Men use work as a drug, and business has not been slow to recognise this. Some sociologists think that the modern business company has replaced family, that bureaucracy is modern kinship. But the company can dump a man in his weakest hour, not rally round to support him. And the background of bureaucracy encourages the more pernicious aspects of male detachment. In the bureaucratic atmosphere, Warren Farrell writes,[6] 'men cannot help but be either emotionally incompetent (unable to handle emotions expressed by others) or emotionally constipated (unable to express their own emotions) or both.' The only secure refuge from the impersonal world of business that can treat an individual as disposable, the only stimulus to join the world of feeling, is from a man's wife and children.

In Sweden a recent report by Marit Paulsen and Sture Andersson, for the Advisory Council on Equality between Men and Women, pinpointed the burdens that men experience in adjusting to the modern world and their changing place in it. Loneliness was one of the chief problems discussed by the men who were interviewed. In a sample of fifty men, all except four said they had no close friends apart from their wives and mistresses; they experienced great difficulty in forming intimate ties, especially with other men, who were treated as old pals but basically looked upon as competitors. At work, most of the men interviewed felt under pressure. At home, they complained that their wives guarded their supremacy, and were unwilling to allow men to enjoy themselves as householders and fathers. Many of the men expressed themselves envious of the emotional rewards that seemed up until now to be the prerogative of motherhood.

Men suffer from too few roles at the moment, while women suffer from a multiplicity of roles. Women are exhausted by the effort to cope successfully with the triangle of husband, children and work, and frequently have to discard one side of the triangle to keep the other two going. Men are running along a straight line, work, that restricts their personalities. They need a wider range of possibilities.

And the children need their father. The advantages of keeping marriage going as the unit for parenting still outweigh the disadvantages heavily. Sexual adventure is something that can be enjoyed, and always has been, far from the marital bed. We may even be able to find a way to institutionalise adultery, to accept it and make it less of a threat. But dual parenting is difficult to achieve in any other setting but marriage. And the particular bonus that mother and father together can give to their children is *character*. Western civilisation has produced its own special personality, toughly individualistic, original, valuing the unique in human perceptions. This particular western character has been moulded in the cauldron of the mother-father-child triangle. Herbert Marcuse[7] for one, regretfully admits that this richly complex western personality cannot survive if the conditions that produced it alter too much, and the strong figures of mother and father are not there to produce passionate reactions in the child. It *is* all a question of upbringing. The most practical modern alternative to family rearing, the kibbutz, does not produce this personality at all, as Bruno Bettelheim[8] has shown. Stability, efficiency, comradeship are all produced by communal upbringing. But a capacity to feel and think with originality and intensity—no.

Parenting is not at all like amiable communal affection. Its essentially luxurious—even hothouse—nature, is most easily understood by examining the detail of child-rearing. Sociologist Elizabeth Newson, with her husband John Newson, has vividly illustrated this in surveys of what parents actually do from day to day with children of a certain age:

> When we were studying four-year-olds, we found that one child in three demanded *and was accorded* a regular bed-time ritual which parents followed exactly every night without fail. The bed-time ritual is only the most common example of idiosyncrasies that parents quite habitually take into account in their everyday dealings with their young children; some children like their shoelaces tied in a particular order,

others have rituals about how an orange or an apple is prepared for their eating, others again set enormous store by sitting in a particular position at table or sharing in a special way in some regular activity of a parent—father's shaving for instance.

Elizabeth Newson was of the opinion that such indulgences strengthened the puny will of the child in his search to establish his individuality and some power over the world. And that hardly anyone but a parent could or would ever be bothered with such tiny but important details. She concluded:[9]

> The crucial characteristic of the parental role is its partiality for the individual child, the best the community can offer is impartiality—to be fair to every child in its care. But a developing personality needs more than that; it needs to know that to someone it matters more than other children; that someone will go to *un*reasonable lengths, not just reasonable ones for its sake. That is the parental role which may well be of the greatest importance of all; and that is the role which society will, I think, find impossible to replace.

To expect one parent on her own to bestow such sumptuous care on a child, or several children, is expecting too much. Not only will she have to sacrifice her whole existence to achieve this; but by doing so she will almost inevitably turn the hothouse temperature up too high. The one parent-child relationship can get far too intense. The best balance, for child and mother, is to have father there too, to be interested in the children in a way that no other male is.

Psychology itself is beginning to show signs of throwing off its reputation as the most mother-dominated of all the sciences. The maternal instinct has begun to be viewed with a colder eye and defined in much more limited ways, to include birth and lactation, and not much more. The essential caring skills of mothers are being pinpointed as learned behaviour, acquired or not acquired in the mother's own childhood; much as the skills of fathering could be taught and learned in fact. The dangerous results of sentimentalising motherhood, have been exposed for all to see when social workers have misguidedly returned a child to its blood mother, even when she has previously ignored or battered her child. The great John Bowlby himself has written in a protest letter to *The Times*[10] that his theories of mother-child attachment have been misunderstood, and that in deciding cases of child placement, 'the tie to be taken into account is always the tie to *the mother figure,* something entirely distinct from the now discredited blood tie'. The mother figure who is important to a child may sometimes be a foster mother; is it unthinkable that in some cases the mother-figure might even be the father?

Children need fathers to hang on to an equal position in the family because mothers, after all, are not saints. Some women reject their children. There are many women whose ignorance and stupidity and malevolence make any observer hope that another adult will be there to dilute the impact on the children. There are women who are just not as warm-hearted as some men. The capacity to love and comfort a small child is not confined to women. It varies between individuals, not between sexes. There are many children who simply rub along best with father; there are some fathers who prefer the domestic world. In growing out of the need for sexual stereotypes, the powerful image of the ever-loving mother needs to be scrutinised more realistically, and the possibility of an ever-loving father find equal acceptance.

But the two-parent family still seems the best bet as a framework that allows the whole intricate network of sexual, intellectual and maternal and paternal needs to be worked out together. It is inside this institution, after all, that most women have found themselves able to embark on the dual role of mother and worker on any sort of ambitious scale. And in its modern transformation, it can and must be adapted to serve more of father's emotional needs, perhaps for the first time.

The immediate technical problem of society seems to be to devise a system of bringing up both boys and girls to look forward to involvement in parenting, to organise to keep two parents at work in the human family, no matter how they divide up their responsibilities, no matter what their combination of careers. Two parents, two jobs and two children should be workable; and there are some who have already found it so.[11] Such a combination is able to offer a wide range of satisfactions to all the individuals involved. The children as well as the parents can grow in such a setting. But it does need everyone to pitch in. At the moment, father's uncertain involvement is both a symptom and a cause of the parental unit falling apart.

Father's current distance from family affairs has not done modern parenting any good. Raising children is falling into disrepute. The awesome task of rearing healthy, sane, cultivated human beings has begun to be dismissed by some as mere 'bottom-wiping' partly because father is not sufficiently involved. Many years ago, Margaret Mead[12] illustrated that most societies divide off certain tasks as masculine or feminine, and that it is the masculine tasks that acquire prestige. In some tribes the men make the grass mats, while the women fish. In others, vice versa. But what never changes is that the male task, whether it is grass-mat making or fishing, is the one that carries status; it is the task that is assumed to need skill and training and is accompanied by important ritual. Whichever task is left to women is soon shrugged off as mere routine drudgery. Men, in short, are the pompous sex. And women, *especially the most ambitious,* acquiesce in this male view of what is and is not important work. Since father stopped spending a lot of time on the job of paterfamilias, what was once considered as the key task of passing on sound values to the young has come to be viewed as mere child-minding. Since father has begun to be considered less vital as a parent, parenting has become a low prestige job. Ambitious and intelligent women who might make a considerable contribution as mothers now feel obliged to avoid much contact with the young, and a woman who is watching her image does not mention children in any company where she wants to be taken seriously. In many circles it has become accepted that it is more important to make it up the ladder to the deputy headship of the department rather than to take three years off to supervise the first years of a new human being.

Men put their work first, the psychologists tell us, through womb envy; they are trying to make up for the fact that they cannot produce children. But for women to be led by men into this reaction is surely the final perversion. Instead of helping men to integrate themselves into the family, a number of women are following men out of it. That parenting is in danger of following fathering, and is beginning to be shrugged off, seems to be increasingly true. 'Children used to be brought up by their parents', declares Urie Broffenbrenner[13] pithily, before accusing the modern English and American family of abandoning their children to the ignorance of the peer group and the doubtful conditioning of television.

Broffenbrenner recalls his old teacher saying of a boy, 'He's a chip off the old block—not because he was knocked off it, but because he knocked around with it.' Today's children, he contends, just do not get a chance to knock around with adults enough. Even at weekends, the parents spend their leisure with other adults, and the children with other children. Typically on Sunday morning, the parents are having drinks in one room and the children are drinking Ribena in another. Fathers and mothers now manage to give their young everything except the basic essentials—a lot of their time and attention. The generation gap has yawned so wide not because the world is moving so swiftly that the older generation is not able to keep up, but because the two generations do not spend enough time together. A recent letter to *Scientific American* queried the need for parents to be with their children a great deal and cited the Israeli kibbutz as a child-rearing device that sidesteps too much parental attention. But, came the rejoinder from another correspondent, in the kibbutz the parents do spend three hours a day with their children, and do nothing else but talk and play with them during that period; that is more time than the average British and American mother and father now manage to find.

Yet any civilisation stands or falls partly through its ability to maintain a continuity of values, by passing on its ideas from one generation to the next. Children cannot teach this to each other. Left to their own devices they struggle against mayhem. In his novel, *Lord of the Flies*, William Golding told a story of a group of English schoolboys wrecked on a desert island who started off trying to operate the rules that they had known at school, but swiftly regressed to barbarism and cannibalism. Urie Broffenbrenner points the moral that without adult supervision, decay soon sets in. 'A society that neglects its children,' he writes, 'however well it functions in other respects, risks eventual disorganisation and demise.'

But if father is having his drinks in the sittingroom, mother, who has been educated now to be very like him, will not sit and drink Ribena in the playroom with the children. To get the generations together means to bring in father too.

The fastest and most cunning device for restoring parenting as a central task of adult life, and one that must be tackled seriously, is to recall father once more to the job. Father alone can confer prestige on the domestic setting. And father's own 'success' can be made to include being a success as a parent. The department head has to understand that it makes a big dent in *his* reputation—not just his wife's—if he has a delinquent son and daughter. But to create the conditions for a revival in fathering and in parenting in general presupposes some shifts in our current preoccupations.

It probably requires some shift of focus from man-woman relationships on to adult-child relationships as a source of general satisfaction and interest in life. It may be, as Margaret Mead has suggested, that a system of 'marriage in two steps' will gradually come into acceptance. Men and women will be able to choose a stimulating, adventurous but childless marriage in which all the adult satisfactions can be pursued and from which divorce is made easy 'by consent', and that another kind of marriage, marriage for parenting, will also be established, in which the couple would set out to get their primary satisfactions from doing a good job by the next generation, and from which divorce would be made very difficult. Some might choose to be parents early and ambitious later; others might prefer to establish themselves as adults first, and think about parenting later. There would be no bar to having both kinds of marriage with the same partner. But such a system would encourage the recognition that parenting is at least what one kind of marriage is for.

At the moment, we seem to spend much of our lives simply pretending that the children are *not there*, an attitude encouraged by popular films and novels where the married lovers are trendily equipped with children apiece, but children who never appear. The divorced mother, played by Glenda Jackson in *A Touch of Class*, was never hampered for a moment by her children; by remaining out of sight and out of mind, they reduced the reality level of the events by several notches. Similarly in Alison Lurie's novel *The War between the Tates*, the offspring of the struggling parents only ever appear as joke horror figures.

Man-woman relations might also benefit if the spotlight were removed for a decade; if for ten years we said 'pax' and stopped the fight and allowed the dust to settle. Marriage and all sexual relationships have been suffering from an overdose of idealism. Attempts to present all 'couple' problems as capable of solution, to encourage the notion that dissatisfaction in marriage can be solved by changing husbands and wives, or by transforming the partner one has, have brought marriage to the edge of ruin. The present high divorce rate is the work of the marriage perfectionists. The more we strive for ideal marriage, the more certainly we shall finish marriage off. Perhaps the way to save marriage is to start expecting less of it. The way to help parenting may be to start expecting and doing more.

Restoring father to the family hearth may also require everyone to work a little less hard. Love and work are the centre of life, but at present we fly too often into the arms of work to mask our difficulties in loving. At least while the children are small, both parents should assert their right to be a little less work-centred. Doing less work may soon be a necessity in our changing economic climate anyway. The rapacious character of our over-producing society has already been halted by recession, and the halt may not be temporary. There may even be a chance to do some radical replanning of the working week to restrict the number of hours that the parents of young children should do. Already many a twelve-hour-a-day man may be forced to experience some leisure and find time to take an interest in the emotional as well as the financial side of his family life. There are some signs that the impact of inflation and unemployment may not be as misery-spreading as most have assumed. On a reduced income, some families now have a chance to read all the books they have bought, listen to all the records they have stacked up and talk to the children they have produced. If the world of work begins to let father down, he can turn to his family. He may be astonished at how much he likes it.

The emotional richness of family life can be profoundly enhanced by social reorganisation, as any family knows that has spent a week in an hotel and marvelled at the hours that unfold for fun or work when room service takes care of all the mundane chores. It isn't practical to move all the parents of pre-school children into hotels for a few years, but there are other devices that can make or break the routine of the day.

The social habits of a number of Continental countries are a pointer. In Italy, Spain and Portugal, partly for reasons of climate, the working day starts early and at 1 o'clock the country halts, not just for the lunch hour, but until 5 o'clock, when work resumes for another three hours. During the long lunch and siesta break, fathers and mothers return from work to their families (the children often do only morning school until their teens). Family lunch becomes an important, lively and much-looked-forward-to event of the day. Work does not suffer, and the family has a chance to survive. The whole system is possible not just because Italian cities are smaller, and long commuting journeys unknown, but also because Italians like life that way. The Norwegians have an even more labour-saving schedule. Breakfast is minimal, and lunch a sandwich at the desk. But work stops throughout the country at 3 o'clock in the afternoon and the one big meal of the day takes place between 4 and 5 o'clock when all the family are together. Cooking is done only once each day and, when it is done, everyone is together to enjoy it. Nor do many Norwegians look kindly on the sort of executive who takes work home in the evenings. As the former chairman of a Norwegian nationalised industry once remarked, 'I can do all my best work in a short six-hour working day. If I have to take anything home after that, I consider it a sign of inefficiency. I should have been able to accomplish it all in working hours.'

It will be up to women to help men redefine life as something more than work and discover that the more they put into being with their children, the more they will get out of it. From the first they have to be as welcoming to men in their family role as they hope men are going to be to them in their work role. There are many women, who relish the power they now exercise in the family, who are thrilled by the knowledge that the children love them best. They may pride themselves on their essentially feminine nature because they do not really wish to compete with men in professional life, but they have fixed for themselves to be victors at home. They are the sort who make sure that the little children are in bed before daddy gets home; the ones who never say, 'I don't know, why don't you ask your father?'

Yet the evidence is that children develop best of all in families where they feel that both parents love them equally, and where they can love both parents equally. Women who want to see father back in the family will understand that he needs to be there to help with the emotional work, not just the washing up. There may be less that he can *do* for his family, but more that he can *be*.

One of the most crucial things for father to be for his family is simply a man. The second half of this century is setting problems for men. 'Man' no longer means 'he who dominates women'. Nor does it always mean 'he who provides'. There are difficulties in any peacetime society that is increasingly scornful of aggression, that has evolved beyond the need for masculine muscle in work or war, and that still must define the male role in ways that will inspire the growing generation of boys. Part of the task of the present generation of fathers is to help solve these questions over the male role in ways that will reassure their sons.

There are some signs that men are beginning to wake up to a definition of father that is not far from the simple Trobriand Island version as 'a man to take the child in his arms'. Fatherhood in some families is beginning to have more of a human and less of a totem aspect. Fathers who have already availed themselves of the 'paternity leave' which a number of organisations now recommend are pleased that 'people are realising that the birth of a baby is a two-person thing now.' An allotted span of time for a young father to be around the house and enjoy the first weeks of his son or daughter's life is beginning to be thought of less as an eccentricity and more as a personal necessity.

Questions of custody in divorce cases are increasingly contested by fathers who cannot accept that they will play little part in their children's lives if they separate from the children's mother. Though the law at the moment is not sympathetic, an increasing number of joint custody decisions, and even custody for the father, are being applied for. Where mother gains custody, some legal enforcement of a father's right to see his children regularly is sorely needed, and is being demanded. Even the unmarried father, a figure whose problems once merely aroused a snigger, is not always now presumed to be a rogue who has no interest in any future but escape. In very rare cases, fathers of illegitimate children have won legal custody of children whom the mothers had preferred to place for adoption.[14]

And some code of behaviour that would allow divorced parents to feel that they are both doing the best possible job in difficult circumstances needs to be worked out. Divorced parents are at present struggling towards new post-divorce conventions that will let them both know where they stand. At the moment many divorced fathers feel that they are damned if they don't see their children, but also damned if they do. As one man relates, 'On some occasions I have taken my children back to my first wife, and they have begun to tell her what a marvellous time they have had with me, and suddenly they have noticed their mother's disapproval. Their faces fall, they look confused and disloyal. I feel vaguely guilty and uneasy.' The divorced father can be left feeling bad about nothing more than the fact that he had a good time with his children.

Everyone can benefit from the re-invention of family roles. Mother is being recognised as a person, and as a person who can think. Father must be recognised as a person, and as a person who can feel. Only when we allow both parents to work out their lives with an equal chance of all-round development can we guarantee that their children grow up in a sexually unprejudiced world. When father or mother dominate, a reaction is produced, and sometimes a violent backlash, in the next generation. Over the last hundred years we have seen the defeat of the tyrannical father; the last thing we should replace him with is a despotic mother. The children have escaped from Mr Barrett; it would be a tragedy to hand them over to Mrs Portnoy.

NOTES

One The Decline of Father

1 *Eros and Civilisation.*
2 *Sex in History.*
3 *Patterns of Infant Care in an Urban Community.*
4 'The Absent Husband in British Middle-Class Families', paper given at BAAS Conference, Guildford, August 1975.
5 'The guilty sex: how American men became irrelevant', *Esquire*, July 1975.
6 *The Descent of Woman.*
7 *Male and Female.*
8 *The Needle's Eye.*

Two Non-Stick Marriage

1 Jessie Bernard, *The Future of Marriage.*
2 *The Dialectic of Sex.*
3 'Are we the last married generation?', *Observer* magazine, 17 September 1967, produced by Maureen Green.
4 'A paternal presence in future family models', in H. A. Otto (ed.), *The Family in Search of a Future.*
5 op. cit.
6 *Kinship and Marriage.*

Three Finding Father

1 'A Cultural Anthropologist's Approach to Maternal Deprivation', in *Deprivation of Maternal Care.*
2 *Kinship and Marriage.*
3 *Male and Female.*
4 ibid.
5 *The Sexual Life of Savages*, p.159.
6 *Marriage and Morals.*
7 *The Female Eunuch.*

162

8 Eva Figes, *Patriarchal Attitudes*.
9 *Male and Female*.
10 *My Mother who Fathered Me*.
11 *Child Care and the Growth of Love*.

Four The Case for Father: Fathers and Sons

1 *Maternal Deprivation Reassessed*.
2 *Father, Child and Sex Roles*.
3 *The Dynamics of Creation*.
4 *The Little Black Schoolhouse: Success and Failure in a Ghetto School*.
5 *The Art of Loving*.
6 *Delinquency and Parental Pathology*.
7 Elizabeth Herzog and Cecilia Sudia, *Boys in Fatherless Families*.

Five The Case for Father: Fathers and Daughters

1 'Interest in persons as an aspect of sex differences in the early years', *Genetic Psychology Monographs*, 55, 1957, pp.287-323.
2 'A girl needs a father', *Listener*, 26 April 1973.
3 *Father, Child and Sex Roles*.

Seven Living with Mother

1 *Boys in Fatherless Families*.
2 ibid.
3 Joseph Goldstein, Anna Freud and Albert Solnit.
4 'From infancy to childhood', *Childhood Education*, March 1963.
5 Dennis Marsden, *Mothers Alone*.
6 *Fatherless Families*.
7 *Motivation and Personality*.
8 In J. C. Flugel's *Man, Morals and Society*, there is a chapter on 'Left and Right as social attitudes' which attributes the conservative, authoritarian, anti-feminist, and sexually inhibited point of view to those who have undergone a strong paternal influence in their upbringing. The opposite radical constellation of social attitudes, the democratic, feminist, and sexually permissive Flugel ascribes to those in revolt against the father figure.

　　Gordon Rattray Taylor, in *Sex in History*, took Flugel's arguments a stage further and constructed the following table of social and political attitudes held by the paternally or the maternally dominated:

Patrist	*Matrist*
1 Restrictive attitude to sex.	1 Permissive attitude to sex.
2 Limitation of freedom for women.	2 Freedom for women.
3 Women seen as inferior, sinful.	3 Women accorded high status.
4 Chastity valued more than welfare.	4 Welfare more valued than chastity.
5 Politically authoritarian.	5 Politically democratic.
6 Conservative; against innovation.	6 Progressive, revolutionary.
7 Distrust of research, inquiry.	7 No distrust of research.
8 Inhibition, fear of spontaneity.	8 Spontaneity, exhibition.
9 Deep fear of homosexuality.	9 Deep fear of incest.
10 Sex differences maximised.	10 Sex differences minimised.
11 Asceticism, fear of pleasure.	11 Hedonism, pleasure welcomed.
12 Father-religion.	12 Mother-religion.

It should be pointed out that in 1972 Gordon Rattray Taylor published *Rethink*, in which he cried 'Whoa' to the present runaway influence of mothers and suggested 'society functions best when there is a balance of father and mother introjections. Middle positions are best'.

9 I am indebted to Elizabeth Herzog and Cecilia Sudia for bringing this marvellous phrase to my attention in *Boys in Fatherless Families*.

Eight Fathering: a Daily Habit

1 'The Pleasures of Life—Children', *Sunday Times*, 8 July 1973.
2 Joel Richman, W. L. Goldthorpe and Christine Simmons, 'Fathers in labour', *New Society*, 16 October 1975.
3 'Marriage as a Human Actualising Contract', in H. A. Otto (ed.), *The Family in Search of a Future*.
4 'How fathers can teach their children sexual equality', *Redbook Magazine*, January 1975.
5 *Bachelor Fatherhood*.
6 *Motivation and Personality*.

Nine Fathering the Mixed Family

1 Jean Seglow *et al.*, *Growing Up Adopted*.
2 'Step-kin relationships', *Journal of Marriage and the Family*, May 1973, pp.283-92.

3   *Divorce and After.*
4   *Fatherhood, a Sociological Perspective.*
5   'Some relationships of step-children to their parents', *Marriage and Family Living*, May 1962, pp.113-21.
6   op. cit.
7   ibid.

Ten The Future for Father

1   National Opinion Poll Survey, 'The Teenagers', *Daily Mail*, 27-30 November 1967.
2   'A paternal presence in future family models', in *The Family in Search of a Future*, ed. H. A. Otto.
3   J. M. Mogey, 'A century of declining paternal authority', *Marriage and Family Living*, 19, 1957, pp.234-9.
4   *The Liberated Man.*
5   'The guilty sex: how American men became irrelevant', *Esquire*, July 1975.
6   op. cit.
7   *Eros and Civilisation.*
8   *The Children of the Dream.*
9   'Towards an Understanding of the Parental Role', in *The Parental Role*, ed. M. L. K. Pringle.
10 29 January 1974.
11 Rhona and Robert Rapoport, *Dual-Career Families.*
12 *Male and Female.*
13 *Two Worlds of Childhood.*
14 Dulan Barber, *Unmarried Fathers.*

Bibliography

Andry, Robert G., *Delinquency and Parental Pathology*, Methuen, 1960.
————, 'Paternal and Maternal Roles and Delinquency', in *Deprivation of Maternal Care: a Reassessment of its Effects*, Geneva, World Health Organisation, Public Health Papers, no.14, 1962.
————, 'Family Patterns with Regard to Paternal Role', in *Foundations of Child Psychiatry*, ed. E. Miller, Pergamon, 1969.
Aries, Philippe, *Centuries of Childhood*, Cape, 1962.
Bach, George R., 'Father fantasies and father-typing in father-separated children', *Child Development*, 17, 1946, pp.63-80.
Barber, Dulan, *Unmarried Fathers*, Hutchinson, 1975.
Benson, Leonard, *Fatherhood, a Sociological Perspective*, New York, Random House, 1968.
Bettelheim, Bruno, *The Children of the Dream*, Thames and Hudson, 1969.
Bernard, Jessie, *The Future of Marriage*, Souvenir Press, 1973.
Biller, Henry B., *Father, Child and Sex Roles*, Lexington, Mass., Heath Lexington Books, 1971.
Bohannan, Paul, *Divorce and After*, New York, Doubleday, 1970.
Bowerman, Charles, and Irish, Donald, 'Some relationships of step-children to their parents', *Marriage and Family Living*, May 1962, pp.113-21.
Bowlby, John, *Maternal Care and Mental Health*, Geneva, World Health Organisation, 1951.
Briffault, Robert, *The Mothers* (abridged and introduced by G. Rattray Taylor), Allen & Unwin, 1959.
Broffenbrenner, Urie, *Two Worlds of Childhood: US and USSR*, Allen & Unwin, 1971.
Burton, Roger V. and Whiting, John M., 'The absent father and cross-sex identity', *Merrill-Palmer Quarterly of Behavior and Development*, 7, 1961. Symposium: The Influence of the Father in the Family Setting.
Carlsmith, Lyn, 'Effect of early father absence on scholastic aptitude', *Harvard Educational Review*, 34, 1964.
Clarke, Edith, *My Mother who Fathered Me*, Allen & Unwin, 1957.
Comfort, Alex, 'A girl needs a father', *Listener*, 26 April 1973.
Cooper, David, *The Death of the Family*, Penguin, 1971.
Department of Health and Social Security, *Report of the Committee on*

One-Parent Families (Finer Report), 2 vols, Cmnd 5629, HMSO, 1974.

Dodson, Fitzhugh, *How to Father*, Los Angeles, Nash Publishing, 1974.

Dominian, Jack, *Marital Breakdown*, Penguin, 1968.

Drabble, Margaret, 'The Pleasures of Life—Children', *Sunday Times*, 8 July 1973.

Duberman, Lucile, 'Step-kin relationships', *Journal of Marriage and the Family*, May 1973, pp.283-92.

Erikson, Erik, *Youth and Crisis*, Faber, 1971.

—————, *Young Man Luther*, Faber, 1972.

English, O.S., and Foster, C.J., *Fathers are Parents Too*, Allen & Unwin, 1953.

Farrell, Warren, *The Liberated Man*, New York, Random House, 1975.

Farson, Richard, *The Future of the Family*, New York, Family Service Association of America, 1969.

Fasteau, Marc Feigen, *The Male Machine*, New York, McGraw-Hill, 1974.

Figes, Eva, *Patriarchal Attitudes*, Faber, 1970.

Finer Report, *see* Department of Health and Social Security.

Firestone, Shulamith, *The Dialectic of Sex*, Cape, 1971.

Flugel, J. C., *Man, Morals and Society: a Psychoanalytic Study*, Duckworth, 1945.

Fox, Robin, *Kinship and Marriage*, Penguin, 1967.

Freud, S., *Leonardo da Vinci*, New York, Random House, 1947.

—————, *Moses and Monotheism*, Hogarth Press, 1951.

Fromm, Erich, *The Art of Loving*, Allen & Unwin, 1957.

Gathorne-Hardy, Jonathan, *The Rise and Fall of the British Nanny*, Hodder & Stoughton, 1972.

Gavron, Hannah, *The Captive Wife*, Routledge & Kegan Paul, 1966.

Goldstein, Joseph, Freud, Anna and Solnit, Albert, *Beyond the Best Interests of the Child*, New York, Free Press, 1973.

Goodenough, E. W., 'Interest in persons as an aspect of sex difference in the early years', *Genetic Psychology Monographs*, 55, 1957, pp.287-323.

Gorer, Geoffrey, *The Americans: a Study of National Character*, Cresset Press, 1948.

Green, Maureen, 'Are we the last married generation?', *Observer Magazine*, 17 September 1967.

Greer, Germaine, *The Female Eunuch*, MacGibbon & Kee, 1970.

Herzog, Elizabeth, and Sudia, Cecilia, *Boys in Fatherless Families*, Washington, US Dept of Health, Education and Welfare, Office of Child Development, 1970.

Hoffman, L. W., 'The father's role in the family and the child's peer group adjustment', *Merrill-Palmer Quarterly*, 7, 1961.

Howells, John G., 'Fathering: modern perspectives', *International Child Psychiatry*, 3, 1969.

Hunt, Morton, *The World of the Formerly Married*, Allen Lane, 1968.

Josselyn, Irene M., 'Cultural forces, motherliness and fatherliness', *American Journal of Orthopsychiatry*, 26, 1956, pp.264-71.

Koch, Stephen, 'The guilty sex: how American men became irrelevant', *Esquire*, July 1975.

Leach, Edmund, *Genesis as Myth and Other Essays*, Cape, 1970.

Lederer, Wolfgang, *Dragons, Delinquents and Destiny*, New York, Psychological Issues series, 4 (3), 1964.

Levett, Carl, 'A Paternal Presence in Future Family Models', in *The Family in Search of a Future*, ed. H. A. Otto.

Lurie, Alison, *The War between the Tates*, Heinemann, 1974.

McFadden, Michael, *Bachelor Fatherhood*, New York, Walker, 1974.

MacFarlane, Jean, 'From infancy to childhood', *Childhood Education*, March 1963.

Mackler, Bernard, *The Little Black Schoolhouse: Success and Failure in a Ghetto School*, New York, Dept of Urban Affairs, Hunter College of the City University of New York, 1969.

Mair, Lucy, *Marriage*, Penguin, 1971.

Malinowski, B., *The Father in Primitive Psychology*, Routledge & Kegan Paul, 1927.

————, *The Sexual Life of Savages*, Routledge & Kegan Paul, 1929.

Marcuse, Herbert, *Eros and Civilisation*, New York, Beacon Press, 1955.

Marsden, Dennis, *Mothers Alone*, Allen Lane, 1969.

Maslow, A. H., *Motivation and Personality*, New York, Harper, 1954.

Mead, Margaret, *Sex and Temperament in Three Primitive Societies*, New York, Morrow, 1935.

————, *Male and Female*, Penguin, 1962.

————, 'A Cultural Anthropologist's Approach to Maternal Deprivation', in *Deprivation of Maternal Care: a Reassessment of its Effects*, Geneva, World Health Organisation, Public Health Papers, no. 14, 1962.

————, 'Marriage in Two Steps', in *The Family in Search of a Future*, ed. H. A. Otto.

Mischel, Walter, 'Father absence and delay of gratification: *cross-cultural comparisons*', *Journal of Abnormal Psychology*, 1961.

Mitscherlich, Alexander, *Society without the Father*, Tavistock Publications, 1969.

Mogey, John M., 'A century of declining paternal authority', *Marriage and Family Living* 19, 1957, pp.234-9.

Morgan, Elaine, *The Descent of Woman*, Souvenir Press, 1972.

Nash, John, 'The father in contemporary culture and current psychological literature', *Child Development*, 36, 1965, pp.261-97.

Newson, Elizabeth, 'Towards an Understanding of the Parental Role', in *The Parental Role*, ed. M. L. K. Pringle, National Children's Bureau, 1972.

Newson, John and Elizabeth, *Patterns of Infant Care in an Urban Community*, Allen & Unwin, 1963.

O'Neill, George and Nena, *Open Marriage*, New York, M. Evans, 1972.

Otto, Herbert A. (ed.), *The Family in Search of a Future*, New York, Appleton-Century, 1970.

Pollack, Otto, 'The outlook for the American family', *Journal of Marriage and the Family*, February 1967, pp.193-205.

Rapoport, Robert and Rhona, *Dual-Career Families*, Penguin, 1971.

Richman, Joel, Goldthorpe, W. L. and Simmons, Christine, 'Fathers in labour', *New Society*, 16 October 1975.

Rodman, Hyman, 'Marital relationship in a Trinidad village', *Marriage and Family Living*, May 1961, pp.166-70.

Russell, Bertrand, *Marriage and Morals*, Allen & Unwin, 1929.

Rutter, M., *Maternal Deprivation Reassessed*, Penguin, 1972.

Satir, Virginia, 'Marriage as a Human Actualising Contract', in *The Family in Search of a Future*, ed. H. A. Otto.

Seglow, Jean, *et al.*, *Growing Up Adopted*, National Foundation for Educational Research, 1972.

Slater, Philip E., 'Towards a dualistic theory of identification', *Merrill-Palmer Quarterly of Behaviour and Development*, 7, 1961.

Symposium: The Influence of the Father in the Family Setting.

Spock, Benjamin, 'How fathers can teach their children sexual equality', *Redbook Magazine*, January 1975.

Storr, Anthony, *The Dynamics of Creation*, Secker & Warburg, 1972.

Tasch, R. J., 'The role of the father in the family, *Journal of Experimental Education*, 20, 1952, pp.319-61.

Taylor, Gordon Rattray, *Sex in History*, Thames and Hudson, 1953.

————, *Rethink: a Para-primitive Solution*, Secker & Warburg, 1972.

Westermarck, E. A., *A History of Human Marriage*, Macmillan, 1922.

Winch, Robert, *Mate Selection*, New York, Harper, 1958.

Wynn, Margaret, *Fatherless Families*, Michael Joseph, 1964.